# Ellacombe Chimes:
## Commemorative Book of Bicentenary 1821-2021

Edited by Mike Gates

With special thanks to Mike Shelley and David Newman
of the Ellacombe Support Group

Bitton Parish History Group

## Acknowledgements

Many people helped to bring about this book, either by contributing to sections or by assisting in the publication. David Newman and Mike Shelley have been supporting the project from the outset and have invaluably contributed sections of the book and assisted in checking and correcting other sections. Laurie Taylor in Sydney and Carl Scott Zimmerman, from Saint Louis sent out invitations across the world. Abi's Grannie applied her artistic skills to the book cover. Jim Heavens produced much of the publicity material. Stephanie Bailey organized our local celebration and proofread the copy. Becky Feather wrote our press releases. Many other people contributed to a team effort by St Mary's Future's Group and Bitton Parish History Group.

Edition 1, June 14, 2012

Published by Bitton Parish History Group
www.Bittonhistory.org.uk

Cover design: Louie, Alex and Abi's Granny

Copyright Bitton Parish History Group
Bitton Parish History Group has asserted its right under the Copyright, Designs and Patents Act of 1988 to be identified as the author of this work.

All rights reserved. This book may not be reproduced or transmitted in any form without the prior written consent of the publisher, except by a reviewer who wished to quote brief passages in connection with a written review or broadcast.

Bitton Parish History Group apologizes in advance for any copyrights that are in place of which it is unaware or which it has been unable to trace.

ISBN 978-1-304-70761-1

# Contents

**THE COMMEMORATIVE EVENT 26 JUNE 2021** ............................................................. 9

**HISTORY OF THE ELLACOMBE CHIMES** ................................................................... 14

**HENRY THOMAS ELLACOMBE (1790-1885)** ............................................................. 23

**ELLACOMBE CHIMES SUPPORT GROUP** ................................................................. 30
    Ellacombe Chimes Support Website ............................................................... 30
    Further Thoughts ............................................................................................. 32
    The Mythical Dangers of Chiming ................................................................... 37

## *WORLDWIDE PARTICIPANTS* ................................................................................ 44

### AUSTRALIA ................................................................................................................ 44
  CANBERRA ............................................................................................................ 44
    The Presbyterian Church of St Andrew ......................................................... 44
    St John's, Canberra ........................................................................................ 45
  NEW SOUTH WALES ............................................................................................. 46
    Holy Trinity, Dubbo ........................................................................................ 46
    Saint Carthages Cathedral Lismore ............................................................... 47
    St John's Church, Darlinghurst, Sydney ........................................................ 48
  QUEENSLAND ....................................................................................................... 49
    St Andrew's Anglican Church, Lutwyche, Brisbane ...................................... 49
  WESTERN AUSTRALIA .......................................................................................... 50
    All Saints Anglican Church, Collie ................................................................. 50
    St John's Anglican Church, Albany ................................................................ 51

### CANADA .................................................................................................................... 52
  BRITISH COLUMBIA ............................................................................................. 52
    Trinity Western University, Langley .............................................................. 52
    St James' Anglican Church, Vancouver ........................................................ 53
  NEWFOUNDLAND AND LABRADOR .................................................................... 54
    St. Thomas' Church, St. John's ..................................................................... 54
  NOVA SCOTIA ...................................................................................................... 55
    St. John's Anglican Church, Truro ................................................................. 55
  ONTARIO .............................................................................................................. 56
    Christ Church (Anglican), Niagara Falls ........................................................ 56
    St. George's Memorial Anglican Church, Oshawa ....................................... 57
    St. John the Evangelist, Peterborough ......................................................... 58
    St. Jude's Church, Oakville ............................................................................ 59
    St. Lawrence Anglican, Brockville ................................................................. 60

- St Paul's, Hamilton ... 61
- Trinity Anglican Church, The "Mountain Chime", Cornwall ... 62
- SASKATCHEWAN ... 63
  - The Anglican Cathedral of St. John The Evangelist, Saskatoon ... 63
  - Knox-Metropolitan United Church, Regina Saskatchewan ... 64
  - Wascana Place, Regina Saskatchewan ... 65

**CHANNEL ISLANDS** ... 66
- GUERNSEY ... 66
  - St Michel du Valle ... 66

**GIBRALTAR** ... 67
- Holy Trinity, Gibraltar ... 67

**INDIA** ... 68
- MAHARASHTRA ... 68
  - Church of the Holy Name, Pune ... 68

**IRELAND** ... 69
- MUNSTER ... 69
  - St Anne's Church, Shandon Bells & Tower, Shandon, Cork ... 69
  - St Michael and all Angels Church Corkbeg ... 70

**NEW ZEALAND** ... 71
- NORTH ISLAND NEW ZEALAND ... 71
  - St Matthew-in-the-City, Auckland ... 71
- SOUTH ISLAND NEW ZEALAND ... 72
  - Sacred Heart Basilica, Timaru ... 72
  - St Mathew's, Dunedin ... 73
  - All Saints Anglican Church, Nelson ... 74
  - Christ Church Cathedral, Nelson ... 75

**SOUTH AFRICA** ... 76
- CAPE TOWN ... 76
  - The Cathedral Church of St George the Martyr, Cape Town ... 76
- EASTERN CAPE ... 77
  - Cathedral of St Michael and St. George, Makhanda ... 77

**USA** ... 78
- COLORADO ... 78
  - St Luke's Episcopal Church, Ft Coffins, Colorado ... 78
- ILLINOIS ... 79
  - Principia College, Elsah ... 79
- MICHIGAN ... 80
  - The Kerrytown Chime Ann Abor ... 80
  - University of Michigan, Michigan ... 81

**U.K. ENGLAND** ... 82

## BATH & NORTH EAST SOMERSET .................................................................................... 82
Bath Abbey ........................................................................................................................ 82
St John the Baptist, Keynsham .......................................................................................... 83
St John the Evangelist Roman Catholic Church, Bath ....................................................... 84
## BRISTOL ........................................................................................................................... 85
Church of The Holy Nativity, Knowle ................................................................................ 85
## CAMBRIDGESHIRE ............................................................................................................ 86
All Saints, St Ives ............................................................................................................... 86
St Margaret's Hemingford Abbots .................................................................................... 87
## COUNTY DURHAM ............................................................................................................ 88
Our Lady Immaculate and St. Cuthbert's R.C. Church, Crook .......................................... 88
## DERBYSHIRE ..................................................................................................................... 89
St Matthew's Church, Hayfield ......................................................................................... 89
St. James, Riddings ........................................................................................................... 90
## DEVON ............................................................................................................................. 91
St Michael and All Angels, Heavitree, Exeter .................................................................... 91
St Margaret's, Topsham .................................................................................................... 92
St David's Church, Exeter .................................................................................................. 93
St. Mary's, Offwell ............................................................................................................. 94
Church of St George, Clyst St George ............................................................................... 95
St Michael the Archangel, Chagford ................................................................................. 96
St Giles' Church, Kilmington ............................................................................................. 97
## DORSET ............................................................................................................................ 98
St Andrew's, West Stafford ............................................................................................... 98
St Mary's Church, Bridport ............................................................................................... 99
St Mary the Virgin Swanage ............................................................................................ 100
Christchurch Priory, Christchurch .................................................................................. 101
## EAST SUSSEX ................................................................................................................... 102
Holy Trinity, Coleman's Hatch ........................................................................................ 102
St Peter's Goldhanger, Maldon ....................................................................................... 103
## GLOUCESTERSHIRE ......................................................................................................... 104
Holy Trinity Church, Drybrook ........................................................................................ 104
## HAMPSHIRE .................................................................................................................... 105
St John's Church, Boldre ................................................................................................. 105
St. Peter & Holy Cross Church, Wherwell ....................................................................... 106
The Abbey Church of St Mary and St Ethelflaeda, Romsey ............................................ 107
## HERTFORDSHIRE ............................................................................................................. 108
St Peter's, Ayot St Peter .................................................................................................. 108
St George's, Anstey ......................................................................................................... 109
## HUNTINGDONSHIRE ....................................................................................................... 110
St. John the Baptist, Holywell-cum-Needingworth ........................................................ 110
## ISLE OF MAN ................................................................................................................... 111
St Thomas', Douglas ........................................................................................................ 111
## KENT .............................................................................................................................. 112
St. Michael and All Angels, Tenterden ............................................................................ 112

- Saints Peter and Paul, Borden ..... 113
- St Michael and All Angels, Hartlip ..... 114
- Sacred Heart Church, Sittingbourne ..... 115
- St Peter's Ightham ..... 116

LANCASHIRE ..... 117
- Saint George's Church, Chorley ..... 117

LEICESTERSHIRE ..... 118
- St Catherine of Alexandria, Burbage ..... 118

LONDON ..... 119
- St Andrew's, Hornchurch ..... 119
- Our Immaculate Lady of Victories ('St.Mary's'), Clapham ..... 120
- St. James's Church, Hampton Hill ..... 121
- St Nicholas Church - Chislehurst ..... 122

MERSEYSIDE ..... 123
- St Peter's, Formby ..... 123
- St Bridget's West Kirby ..... 124

NORFOLK ..... 125
- Our Lady Saint Mary, South Creake ..... 125
- St. Mary's Church Baconsthorpe ..... 126
- All Saint's Old Buckenham ..... 127

NORTH YORKSHIRE ..... 128
- All Saints' Bolton Percy ..... 128
- St Mary's Goathland, Whitby ..... 129
- St Helens Parish Church, Wheldrake ..... 130
- St James the Great, Baldersby St James ..... 131
- St Wilfrid's Burnsall ..... 132

NORTHAMPTONSHIRE ..... 133
- St Giles Church, Desborough ..... 133

NORTHUMBERLAND ..... 134
- Holy Trinity, Whitfield ..... 134

OXFORDSHIRE ..... 135
- St. Leonard's Church, Waterstock ..... 135
- The Orthodox Church of St Nicholas the Wonderworker, Marston, Oxford ..... 136
- St Michael at the North Gate, Oxford ..... 137
- St. Leonard's Church, Waterstock ..... 138

SOUTH GLOUCESTERSHIRE ..... 139
- St Mary's - Bitton ..... 139

SURREY ..... 140
- St Philomena's Catholic High School for Girls founded by the Daughters of the Cross, Carshalton 140
- St Mathew's, Surbiton ..... 141

WARWICKSHIRE ..... 142
- St James the Great Church, Snitterfield ..... 142
- St Mary's Warwick ..... 143
- St Peter's Catholic Church, Leamington Spa ..... 144

WEST SUSSEX ..... 145

St Wilfrid's Haywards Heath .................................................................................. 145
St Bartholomew, Rogate ...................................................................................... 146

# U.K. SCOTLAND .................................................................................................. 147
STIRLING AND FALKIRK .......................................................................................... 147
Dunblane Cathedral ........................................................................................... 147
PEEBLESHIRE ....................................................................................................... 148
Peebles Old Parish Church, Peebles ................................................................. 148

# UK WALES ............................................................................................................ 149
CAERPHILLY ........................................................................................................ 149
St Martin's Church, Caerphilly .......................................................................... 149
CARDIFF .............................................................................................................. 150
Llandaff Cathedral ............................................................................................. 150
CONWY ............................................................................................................... 151
St Cynbryd's Church, Llanddulas ....................................................................... 151
VALE OF GLAMORGAN ....................................................................................... 152
St Andrew's, Dinas Powys ................................................................................. 152
St Augustine's, Penarth ..................................................................................... 153

## Location of Participants Featured in this book

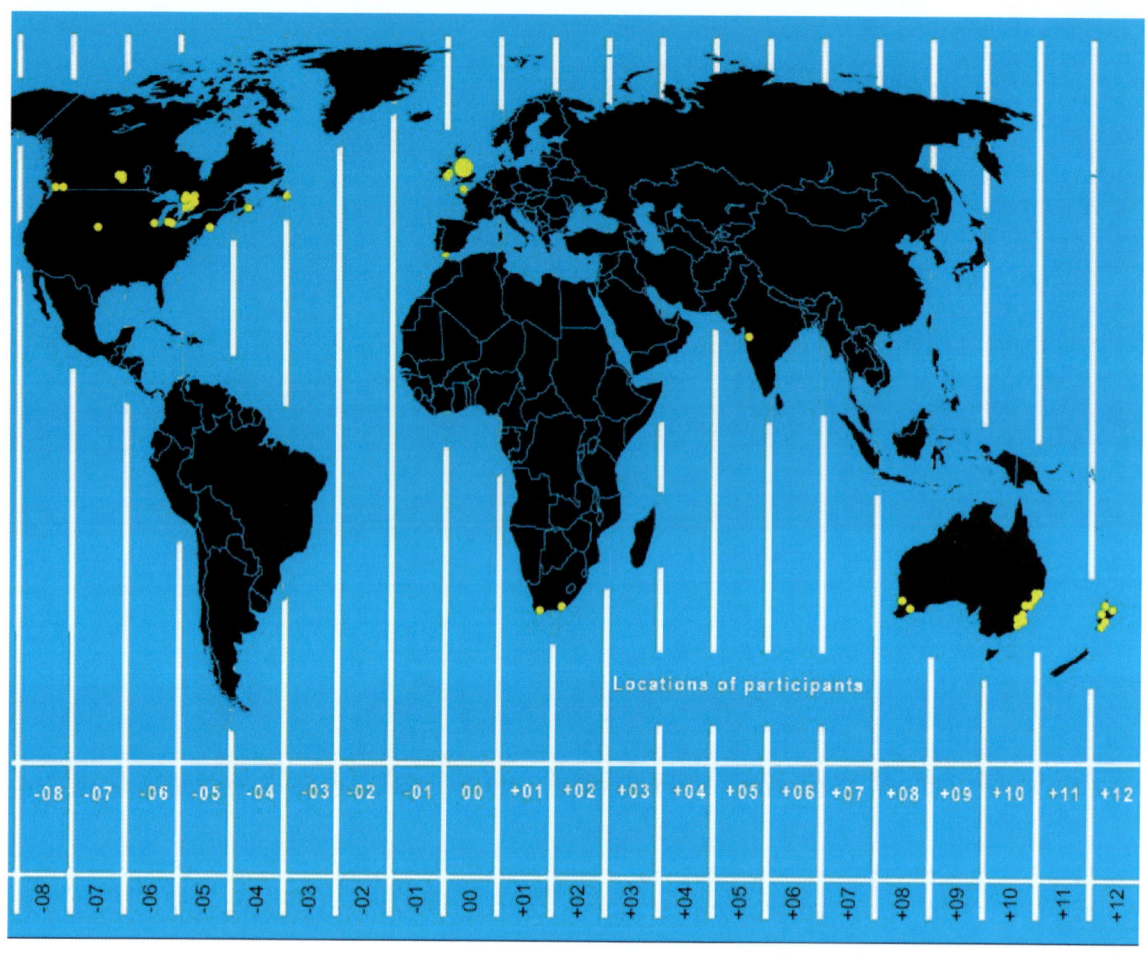

# THE COMMEMORATIVE EVENT 26 JUNE 2021

## The Worldwide Event

A truly worldwide celebration happens on 26th June with bells that will ring throughout the world, played at noon local time in each location, across four continents and eleven time zones, starting in New Zealand and finishing in Vancouver, Canada, 17 hours after they first started.
At the time or going to press, at least 120 churches and towers will be taking part.

## From New Zealand to Australia

The celebration starts at noon in New Zealand at St Matthew-in-the-City, Auckland. Five other churches will be ringing bells across New Zealand. Joining in will be Nelson Cathedral which is where every year the Ellacombe Chimes are used to celebrate the return of the godwits after their non-stop flight from Alaska - the longest flight of any bird. Two hours later the bells will be heard from locations in Australia.

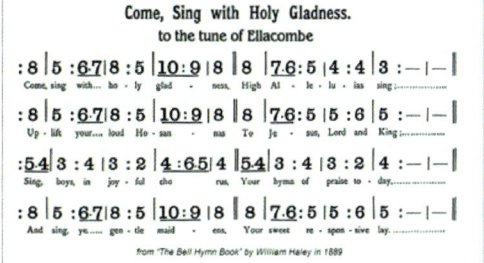

Ellacombe hymn on 9 bells

*St Matthew-in-the-City, Auckland*

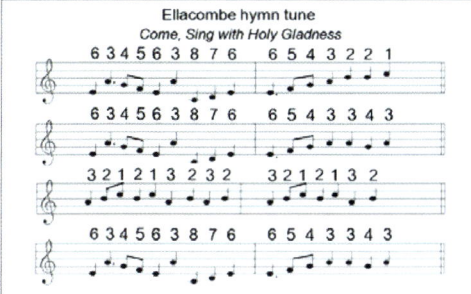

Ellacombe Hymn on 8 bells

Ellacombe Hymn on 6 bells

One of the most enthusiastic supporters of the celebration is Laurie Alexander from St John's Darlinghurst, Sydney, who sent out many invitations to friends. He plans to ring at noon and have someone on the door giving out brochures, to tell passers by and visitors about the event, and later, even invite some locals to come up to the tower to give the bells a bit of a ring. They have had local tower days before and all ages love it!

At Holy Trinity, Dubbo, New South Wales, they plan to follow the noon performance by an organ recital with a newly purchased organ.

**Next Stop India followed by South Africa and Gibraltar**

The next stop will be Pune in India from the Church of the Holy Name, also known as Pavrita Naam Delaya. This is a unique church that has been in use every day since being built. Its clock tower scales to a height of 130 feet and has 8 bells cast by Taylor and Sons.

One hour before British Summer Time, bells will be heard from South Africa and Gibraltar. At the Cathedral of St Michael and St. George, Makhanda, the bells will be rung at what is thought to be the first ring of bells to be installed in Africa. The celebration will then be taken on to the UK and Ireland where over 70 churches and towers will take part.

**Reaching their birth place**

St Mary's Bitton is where the Ellacombe Chimes apparatus was first invented 200 years ago. Bitton Parish History Group has worked with St Mary's Future's committee on the event which will help publicise plans for the development of the church so that the church may become an even more useful community asset as well as a place of worship. The local primary school, The Meadows, will be displaying flags of participating countries, bunting bells, posters of the church, as well as the children's idea of rules and regulations for bellringers. There will be prizes, and local families will picnic as they listen live to the bells rung by our own ringers and those around the world.

*St Mary's Bitton*

At St James the Great Church in Snitterfield, Warwickshire they plan an Open Day to celebrate the Ellacombe bicentenary and dedicate the newly restored Bells of St James. An electronic time capsule to include some original scores for the Ellacombe will be placed in the Bell Tower to ensure the tradition continues.

The Church of St George, Clyst St George in Devon is where Revd. Ellacombe spent the last thirty-five years of his life. St Clyst's celebration will include John Langabeer chiming the apparatus at noon to summon people to meet for a village picnic at the village hall. The pandemic permitting, they hope to have a bar, some stalls and children's entertainment there. As the church is a short distance away, they have a life size facsimile of Ellacombe at the church door to welcome people.

10

John, who will be chiming at intervals from noon, will supervise anyone wishing to have a go on the apparatus.

Russian church bells will be heard at the Orthodox Church of St Nicholas the Wonderworker, at Oxford, where, by tradition, the bells have and will be chimed. The ringers will perform their usual highly complex patterns of chimes in various rhythmic arrangements, or zvons. Traditionally, the ringer chimes the bells from a mechanism within the bell chamber, level with the clappers. As the tower and bell chamber at St Nicholas are small and inaccessible, a compromise solution to the problem of how to chime the bells as authentically as possible was found. An electric ringing mechanism with a series of pre-programmed zvons had been supplied by the bell foundry in Russia, but the church council had a strong preference for manual chiming, so an Ellacombe Chimes mechanism was installed, believed to be the only Ellacombe apparatus in use in an Orthodox church in the UK, and possibly in the world.

Some churches and towers have arranged special programmes. Ollie Watson at Holy Trinity, Coleman's Hatch, who has chimed the bells each Sunday for the service during the pandemic, has planned a special one-hour long recital to be rung starting at noon. The hymns and music have been specially chosen to cater for everyone. Members of the public are invited to sit outside and listen. The following programme is planned:

God Save the Queen
The Ellacombe Hymn
Abide with Me
All Things Bright and Beautiful
Guide Me Oh Thou Great Redeemer
Praise My Soul the King of Heaven
Tell Out My Soul
Jerusalem

I Vow to Thee My Country
White Cliffs of Dover - Vera Lynn
Hey Jude - The Beatles
Over the Rainbow - Israel Kamakawiwo'ole
Can't help falling in love - Elvis Presley
I want to break free – Queen
Yesterday - The Beatles

A commemorative booklet has been produced by Saint George's Church, Chorley, Lancashire to celebrate the bi-centenary, available as a free electronic download from the Church website. The Ellacombe Chimes will be played at noon by the Tower Captain, Dr Victoria Gibson, and live streamed on the Church YouTube Channel and Social Media platforms. A special peal has been composed for the occasion and a service of commemoration will take place in the Tower.

At St Andrew's, Hornchurch, Essex, the performances planned for the bicentenary celebrations are as follows:
- Morning Has Broken – Michelle Stephenson
- Oranges and Lemons – Adam Carpenter
- All Things Bright and Beautiful – Valerie Swain
- Musical Changes – Gavin Carpenter
- Ellacombe Hymn – John Church
- Scotland The Brave – Helen Carter
- Z Cars Theme – Tony Ammerlaan
- Abide With Me – Pauline Murray
- Hand Bell Dancing – Clive Stephenson

*The Hornchurch Chiming team for 2021 celebrations*

St Helen's Wheldrake, York, are planning to join the celebration on their Ellacombe Chime at noon. Information will go out to the village in their pew news to explain what is happening and a selection of tunes will be rung for 30 minutes. The Church will have the doors open back and front, and the tower door will be open so the sound will come into the church. There will be chairs in the churchyard and the audience will be encouraged to choose tunes from a repertoire of 150 arrangements.

**Ireland**

The celebrations will then cross over the Irish Sea to St Michael & All Angels, Corkbeg and St Anne's church, Shandon, with its 8 bells made famous by the song "The Bells of Shandon" by Francis Sylvester Mahony.

'With deep affection and recollection
I oft times think of those Shandon bells,
Whose sound so wild would in the days of childhood,

Fling round my cradle their magic spells'

## North America

Three and a half hours later the bells will strike out on the coast of North America, first at St John's Newfoundland, two and half hours behind GMT.

At Principia College in Elsah, IL a concert performed by the well known Director/Carillonist, Carlo van Ulft, will be held at 10:30am CST on 26th June, accessible at https://principia-edu.zoom.us/j/7773231187.

*Carlo van Ulft*

The University of Michigan will feature a special performance. Their carillon studio students, Xiaoying Pu, Abigail Findley, Yiqing (Mitty) Ma and HyoJin (Jenna) Moon are featuring:
- Historically Interesting Changes, 10 Bells by Percival Price
- Duet Russian Traditional Pearls by Olesya Rostovkaya
- Set of European Hymns by Sally Slade Warner
- Prelude for Bells by Gladys Watkins.

*Jenna Moon (Doctoral candidate in Sacred Music) and*

Chloe Thiessen a graduate of TWU, Langley, Canada, composed an arrangement of Ellacombe's tune that is now part of the campus repertoire.

Having travelled across Canada and the USA, the celebrations will finally arrive at St James Anglican Church, Vancouver, British Columbia, 17 hours after they started.

The bells will have crossed four continents with at least 120 participants in eleven different time zones.

The Covid pandemic may well cast a shadow on celebrations for the day, in part due to different restrictions in place in some countries and due to the uncertainty of an evolving situation. However, this will not have too great an impact on the ability for bells being joyfully rung using the Ellacombe apparatus.

*St James Anglican, Vancouver*

13

# HISTORY OF THE ELLACOMBE CHIMES

**The Invention**

The Ellacombe apparatus is a device that enables one person to ring all the bells in the tower using a rope which is connected to a series of hammers which strike the bells. Each of the bells is struck while the bell is static instead of the bells being rotated and was devised so that all the bells could be rung by one person without involving a band of ringers. The Ellacombe Chimes have made a significant impact on the enjoyment of the sound of bells the world over.

The apparatus was invented by the Revd. Henry Thomas Ellacombe while Curate at St Mary's Church, Bitton (located between Bristol and Bath).

Revd. Ellacombe devised the mechanism so that all the bells could be rung by one trusted person without involving a band of ringers.

Because the mechanism strikes stationary bells with hammers it does not have the same sound as full circle ringing due to the absence of Doppler effect caused by the bells not rotating.

*H.T. Ellacombe in 1817*

The mechanism has a frame which is located in the vestry or the bell-ringing room of the church. When in use, the ropes are taut and pulling one of the ropes towards the player will strike the hammer against the bell. For normal full circle ringing, the ropes are slackened to allow the hammers to drop away from the moving bells.

Revd Ellacombe was the editor of the bell ringing column of a church periodical called "Church Bells", and he was not slow to criticise the actions of bell ringers who did not ring exclusively for church services. A particular target was "prize ringing", where teams from different churches competed for a prize for the best ringing, usually accompanied by a social event. An example was in 1875 when he weighed in with a diatribe against a ringing competition at Slapton in Devon, when he wrote, "We blame the Vicar and churchwardens for allowing the bells to be so prostituted for the benefits of a publican's pocket…" (John Eisel, The Blackawton Boys, The Ringing World 2017, edition No 5519, p. 103).

It was not until Ellacombe presented a paper on bells for the Bristol Architectural Society, on Dec. 10, 1849 that we have evidence of the strength of Ellacombe's feelings about the disruption from ringers. He later published this together with an appendix as 'Practical Remarks on Belfries and Ringers' in 1850. He starts off the work with the statement:

'Reared in a country parsonage, and close to a peal of eight bells, as musical and as well rung as any in the kingdom, it has been my lot from childhood to have seen much of the practices in a country belfry. They had better, I grieve to say, be passed over in silence ; for such things as I remember to have seen and heard would hardly be tolerated in a village ale-house ; and yet the ringers were considered respectable, honest men in their way, and had the honour many of them of being the ringers of the Cathedral bells in the adjoining city, where fifteen men were required; and it was a well-known fact that, as a body, a more drunken set of fellows could not be found.'

*St Mary's, Bitton, home of the invention*

He also complained that scarcely any of the ringers attended services and that he would see the bell ringers waiting in the churchyard until the service was over and not until everyone had left that they would 'strike out a merry peal'. He eventually managed to get hold of the keys to the tower which before had enabled the ringers to have uncontrolled admission to the belfry when they pleased.

In this publication we first see Ellacombe's own description of his apparatus:

'This may be effected either by heavy hammers to strike outside on the " bridge" of the bells, like those of a clock ; or by fixing light hammers or balls, portioned in size, and in length of lever, to each bell, and so arranged to work on an axis as to strike on the inside just where the clapper strikes, and when not in use, to drop down, so as to be quite clear of the swing of the bell when rung. This mode is more simple than the outside hammers, for which there is often little or no room. A cord, or "sash line" fastened at the end of the lever, may be guided by pulleys to a given point in the church, where the ends are tied, when used, to a fixed horizontal bar. This bar should be about three feet from the floor; and about two feet above it there should be the last set of pulleys, arranged in a row about three inches apart the pulleys should not be less than four inches in diameter. Care should be taken to pull the lines down, so that the hammer or ball may be adjusted above within a few inches of the bell. With such an arrangement one person may easily do all the work: the lines must be untied when he has finished, otherwise the bells cannot be rung if required. In this way the chiming is done at Bitton; and by this simple method,

'To call the folk to church in time
One little boy six bells can chime'

indeed, any number might thus be chimed.'

**The Intellectual Property**

The invention of the chiming apparatus is attributed to Ellacombe, but the concept at least should be attributed to Sam Watts. Born in 1796, he was registered in the 1841 Census as a carpenter living in the village of Bitton. Perhaps the apparatus should have been called the Watts Chimes!"

Ellacombe mentions Watts and the invention of the apparatus in his 'The History of the Parish of Bitton' (Ellacombe, H.T.; W Pollard, 1881, Vol 1)

> 'In the basement of the tower is a manual, within a case, for chiming the bells for service by means of a hammer striking the inside of the bells above. This was set up in 1822. The method was suggested to me by Sam Watts, a clever workman, and is supposed to be the first thing of the sort. Since that time the same contrivance has been set up in about two hundred towers. It is so arranged above as not to interfere with the gear for ringing. The lines being brought down to the floor, a child may easily call the people to the Services of the day. Before this the tenor bell only was tolled, which has a melancholy sound, instead of the sweet, mellow, and subdued tones which the bells cheerily throw out when they are chimed. The difficulty of getting a sufficient number of hands to do this daily, or it may be only on Sundays and Saints' days, with unbroken regularity for both services, is often found to be impracticable, especially in country places; and therefore, this simple contrivance is very valuable to all who consider chiming one of the most legitimate uses of bells. It is available for any number of bells, and lately it has been fixed at Worcester Cathedral for chiming the twelve bells for the daily Services. The chiming gear being distinct from the clappers, it does away with the lazy practice, which is so common, but so destructive, of "clocking" the bells, or tying ropes to the clappers, by which so many fine bells have been cracked. The place for the manual should be the ground floor of the tower, which is also the proper place for the ropes to be brought down for the ringing.'

We have no documentary evidence of the invention other than the illustration appended to 'Bells and Ringers' by Ellacombe 29 years later in 1850, which would make a definitive case for the originator of the invention.

Included in the illustration is the wording 'The Author's Contrivance for Chiming' and so Ellacombe certainly claimed to be the inventor. It is highly likely that Ellacombe would have made sketches or drawings of the contraption in 1821. He made prolific sketches of architectural features for the vicarage and St Mary's church. No doubt, given Ellacombe's admission that the original idea came from Watts, if this was a current day invention, both Ellacombe and Watts would be listed as the joint patent holders.

> **ST MARY'S CHURCH BITTON**
>
> **BELLRINGERS' RULES**
>
> 1. IN FUTURE THERE IS TO BE ONLY ONE BELLRINGING TEAM.
> 2. THE BELFRY KEY TO BE KEPT IN THE CHURCH WARDEN'S HOUSE AND NOT TAKEN AWAY WITHOUT HIS CONSENT.
> 3. IN CHURCH SERVICES, NO BELLRINGER IS TO REFUSE TO RING OR RING BADLY JUST BECAUSE THE FEE IS TOO SMALL.
> 4. PUNISHMENT FOR BEERISH BELFRY BEHAVIOUR, LIKE SQUABBLING, SWEARING OR EXCESSIVE DRINKING, SIX MONTHS EXCLUSION FROM THE BELFRY.
>
> SIGNED
>
> H T ELLACOMBE

*Fig.1: Bell Ringers' Rules of 1799*

Ellacombe instigated a firm set of rules for the bell ringers, to which each ringer had to pledge compliance before being allowed to join (as well as being able to raise and fall his bell in proper time and place, and ring one peal of changes). There had in fact been rules in St Mary's Bitton since 1799 (fig. 1) but these were clearly not abided by, at least when Ellacombe became curate in 1817. The rules can still be seen as at 2021 in the ringing room of St Mary's.

In 'Practical Remarks on Belfries and Ringers' (1850), Ellacombe makes clear that he set much store by insisting on their compliance as essential to successful control of the bell ringers. Astutely, he surmised that control of money (which he saw as the root of all evil) paid to bell ringers was the means to have the utmost influence on them. The initial six of the twenty-nine rules are shown here:

ST. MARY'S CHURCH, BITTON. RULES FOR THE RINGERS.

WE, the undersigned company of Ringers of the parish of Bitton, by and with the consent and approbation of our Vicar and Church-wardens, have agreed to the following rules and resolutions: namely,

FIRST, and chief of all, We resolve to be a respectable body of men, as well as good Ringers and to give no occasion, by our conduct, to any person to speak against us, nor to bring a disgrace on the church in which we are connected officials. Neither will we desire to take into our company any who are of low life and character idle, drunken fellows, and sabbath-breakers; for we acknowledge that the belfry is part of the church, and that the Ringers, being officers of the church, should bear a good character: and this is what we will endeavour to promote.

II. "We agree to have a Treasurer, who shall hold our moneys till the end of the year, and the same person shall be the foreman of our company; and he is to see that these rules are observed, and the forfeits hereafter mentioned put in force, and deducted out of the moneys given to us; and they are to be regularly entered in a book to be kept by him, and divided equally among the ringers at the end of the year. And if our treasurer and foreman does not do this, the majority of us shall elect another.

III. We now agree that G. B. shall be our treasurer and foreman.

IV. When the bells are to be rung for a marriage, or any other special occasion, the foreman shall give notice thereof to the Ringers.

V. Every Ringer who shall not attend at all on such occasions shall have no share of what is given and shall also forfeit one shilling; unless he is prevented by sickness, sufficient to disallow him from working (provided timely notice has been given); every Ringer so absent shall be entitled to half a share. And every Ringer, having had notice, is to be at the tower by the time the bells are raised up, or forfeit sixpence. And if he does not remain till the ringing is all over he is to forfeit his whole share; unless the majority present give him leave to go off.

VI. When there is ringing more than once on the same day, if any Ringer does not attend at each time, he is not to have his full share; but only a part, in proportion to his attendance.

We can deduce from the rules that it may not have been so much the 'drunken and unruly' behaviour of the ringers that led to the invention of the chimes, but rather that the ringers were motivated by money and so out of Ellacombe's control. The rules have 24 clauses, 16 of which are about money or payment.

Most of the parishioners in Bitton in the early nineteenth century would have struggled to provide for their families and so would be desperate for extra cash. Any money from a task such as bell ringing was certainly much easier than descending a mine shaft at 5 am. The local employment was agriculture, hat-making, the brass mill and coal mining. The most lucrative employment was coal mining. We know from Children's Employment Commission on Mines in 1842, some two decades later, that in 1841 there were eight boys under the age of 13 at the local Golden Valley Colliery. They worked from five o'clock in the morning till one p.m., working a vein of about two and half feet. Most of them could read a little and attended

Sunday-school. At the near-by Hole Lane Pit at Oldland Common about forty boys were under the age of 13, the youngest had started at the age of just six-years. The Children's Employment Commission, interviewed hundreds of children in coalmines, works and factories. Its findings, reported in 1842, were deeply shocking. Particularly heart rending is the account of John Harvey who was a carter in the local Crown Pit at Warmley. He was described at the age of 13 as 'half-fed, half clothed and stunted in growth. He seldom had as much as he could eat. He did not go to Sunday school because he had no clothes other than his work clothes'.

Clearly then, the possibility of earnings from ringing bells was highly attractive and every opportunity to ring bells, for example: for the local publican, or for a celebration such as a birthday, would have been highly tempting.

It was not only Ellacombe's advocacy of rules for bell ringers that furthered belfry reform, but also the influence that he exerted through his writing and the extensive visits he made to churches. From 1871 until his death, he was also influential through his editing of the "Church Bells" magazine.

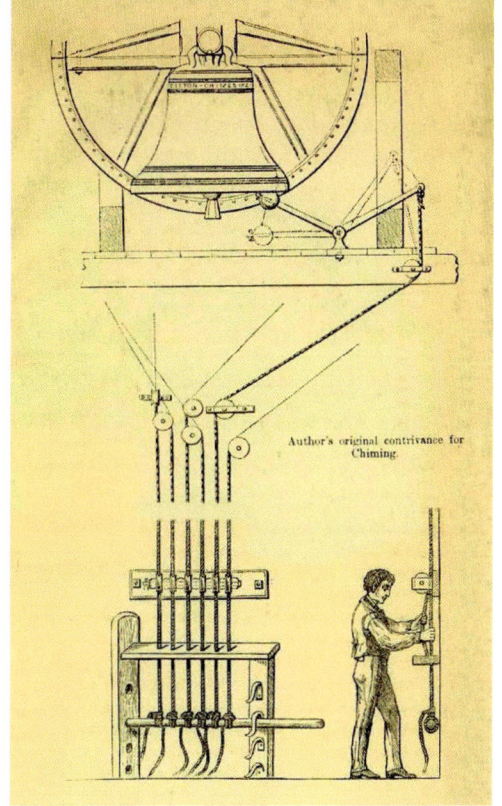

Author's original contrivance for Chiming.

At the Third annual meeting of the Central Council of Church Bell Ringers held in 1893 and reported in Church Bells, April 7, 1893, page 360., Canon Erskine Clarke, the Editor of Church Bells, said that he was glad to have been able to do something to raise change-ringing from being looked on only as a kind of sport to one which was regarded as a form of Church work. He said that he must candidly admit that what 'Church Bells' had done was rather an accident of the title of the paper. The paper was started in 1871 to be an organ of moderate Churchmanship, and the name was chosen simply as a popular one; but it was suggested that belfry reform was needed, and so the venerable Mr. Ellacombe, then rector of Clyst St. George, undertook to edit a column on 'Bells and Bell-ringing.' He was glad that ringers now had an organ of their own, which could give more space than he could afford. He hoped that 'Bell News' would flourish, while the small section which he was able to spare in Church Bells would introduce the ringing science to many readers who would not see a special organ.

19

Many of the towers which had Ellacombe Chimes installed in the nineteenth century have later had them removed, often leaving holes in the ceiling. Additionally, a number have not been maintained and so cannot readily be played nowadays. While chiming is a single person activity, ringers often prefer the team activity and social interaction of full circle ringing. When some towers had additional bells or the frames were replaced, the chimes were sometimes not upgraded. In some towers heavier bells were frequently left in the up position thus reducing the effort and preparation time.

**William Hayley – 'The Bell Hymn Book'**

The impact of the Revd. Ellacombe's invention, and recognition that it could be used to play tunes, must have been significantly enhanced by the publication in 1889 of William Haley's book entitled: "The Bell Hymn Book". It is in effect a beginner's guide to playing hymns on the Ellacombe Chimes. Haley wrote these words in the introduction to the book:

> "The following pages have been compiled, believing that the labour bestowed thereon will tend to supply a long-felt want, and to make the Chimes of the Village or Parish sound their notes in such succession as shall lead, perhaps, to higher thoughts and desires than simple permutation, and changing positions".

The book then has 9 pages of 'instructions' for beginners (albeit in a somewhat dated writing style), followed by the music for 143 hymns using his system of notation, with 2 tunes for 5 bells, 6 for 6 bells, 24 for 8-bells, 20 for 10-bells, 44 for 12-bells.

William Haley was the son of Henry Haley, who was well recognised in the ringing world at the time. By the age of 23 he had composed and called his first peal - Stedman Caters. He also rang and called many peals on hand-bells and organised the first ever pe

al of Stedman Triples on handbells in 1853. He was one of a party of ringers who travelled to the USA in 1850 and called the first ever peal there of Grandsire Triples in Christ Church, Philadelphia.

William Haley was employed as a bell tuner with John Warner & Sons Ltd., who were bell founders at Cripplegate, London and so he would also been very knowledgeable on all aspects of bell ringing. His company also made handbells Carillons and Ellacombe Chimes equipment.

At the dedication of new bells at St Luke's in Deptford in 1877 William Haley played tunes on the bells using a temporary Ellacombe chimes rack set up within the church. Both father and son took part in the dedication ring of the new St Paul's Cathedral ring of twelve in 1878.

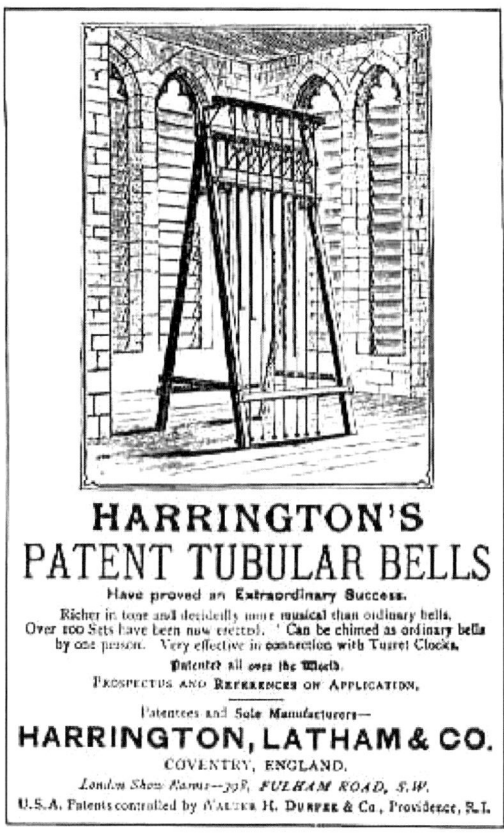

William Haley's expertise, his involvement with chiming and the publication of the book could well have gone some way to overcome the schism that existed for more than a century between those clerics who suffered from undisciplined ringers and hence advocated chiming in their churches, and those ringers who were disciplined, sober and dedicated to the art of change ringing and methods.

## Harrington's Tubular Bells

Tubular bells may have been used in France as early as the 1850s or 1860s, but in the English-speaking world, they got their start when John Harrington, of Coventry, Warwickshire, England, patented a clock-chime of tubular bells in that country in 1884. It was an immediate success, winning gold medals at Paris in 1885 and at Liverpool in 1886.

Harrington's Tubular bells developed and sold around the world complete with Ellacombe Chimes between 1890s and 1930, have had a significant impact on the use of Chimes. Several hundred of their systems were installed in churches and public buildings throughout the world and many are still in working order, because they were built with metal frames and put much less strain on the tower.

Most tubular bells were constructed by Harrington's of Coventry between 1890s and the 1920s using their patented design. John Harrington had developed and patented the design as early as 1884. The quality and tone of the chimes earned him a gold medal at the 1885 Paris World Fair. A USA patent was granted in 1888.

It is known that Harrington's installed several hundred of their tubular bells in churches and other buildings around the world Many are in good working order and use Ellacombe frames.

In 1894 Walter Durfee of Rhode Island in the USA ceased importing Harrington's tubular tower bells and began manufacturing them under his own name, continuing to use Ellacombe frames. Later Durfee became the president of the United States Tubular Bell Company which also used Ellacombes for their bells. Some of these still exist in North America but the Ellacombe frame is sometimes known as the 'taut-rope chiming rack' or just 'taut-rope rack'.

There are now over 600 Ellacombe Chimes around the world with 430 of those being in the UK. Whether they should be called Ellacombes or Ellacombe-Watts, they continue to be a great asset to the enjoyment of the sound of bells and chimes the world over.

*St Wilfrid's Church, Hayward's Heath*

Sources:
Bitton Parish History Group http://www.bittonhistory.org.uk, accessed 23 May 2021
*Children's Employment Commission, First Report of the Commissioners*: Mines, HMSO, 1842
Ellacombe Chimes Support http://www.churchside1.plus.com, accessed 23 May 2021
Ellacombe, H.T., *The History of Parish of Bitton*, Wm. Pollard, Exeter, 1883
Ellacombe, H.T., *Practical Remarks on Belfries and Ringers* Bristol, 1850, 4th edit. 1876
Eisel, John, *The Blackawton Boys*, published in The Ringing World 2017, edition No 5519, p. 103
Hill, A. W. *Henry Nicholson Ellacombe: a memoir* (1919)
Mozley, T., *Oxford Dictionary of National Biography*, Reminiscences, chiefly of Oriel College and the Oxford Movement, 1 (1882), 75–81
https://www.whitingsociety.org.uk, accessed 23 May 2021.

# HENRY THOMAS ELLACOMBE (1790-1885)

## Vicar of St Mary's Bitton

Henry Thomas Ellacombe was an extraordinarily energetic and capable man who was also kind and compassionate to his parishioners. He was curate of St Mary's from 1817 to 1835 and then vicar till 1850. He published The History of the Parish of Bitton (2 vols. 1881, 1883); he was perhaps the foremost campanologist of his time; he restored his church and built three others locally; he embarked on much reform in Bitton and was also a renowned gardener.

His son, Canon Henry Nicholson Ellacombe, vicar of Bitton from 1850 until his death in 1916, continued these interests, and became a well-known gardener. His garden was famous for its collection of rare plants, an endeavour started by his father.

*Rev H.T. Ellacombe, Illustration: Bath Central Library/ Bath In Time*

## Family Background

H.T. Ellacombe changed the spelling of his name from Ellicombe rather than Ellacombe as he considered this to be the more correct rendering, but other members of the family retained the original spelling. He was born at Alphington, Devon, on 15 May 1790, the second of seven sons of William Ellicombe (d. 1831), rector of Alphington, and his wife, Hannah, née Rous.

*Illustration: St Mary's Church at the time H.T.Ellacombe was Curate/Vicar*

He graduated from Oriel College, Oxford with a BA in 1812. After studying engineering at Chatham dockyard under (Marc) Isambard Brunel, he returned to Oxford in 1816 to prepare for ordination in the Anglican ministry, and became curate of Cricklade, Wiltshire. He was married three times. His first marriage, on 3 April 1818 at Rochester, was to Anne Nicholson (d. 1825), daughter of a government contractor. They had five daughters and one son. He married, second, on 11 September 1827, Ann (d. 1831), daughter of George Bridges of Ashton Lodge, Gloucestershire. He married his third wife Charlotte (d. 1871) on 6 January 1835, at Shillingford, Devon, daughter of the Revd R. Palk Welland.

**Rebuilding churches**

Ellacombe was extremely energetic as a parish priest, restoring St Mary's in 1822, and building three other churches in the district, where there was a large population of dissenters.

The first of these was the Church of the Holy Trinity on Kingswood Hill, which was the first church built by the Million Fund Commissioners, and was consecrated in 1821. In Oldland an Early English chapel was rebuilt as St. Anne's Oldland in 1830, which in 1861 led to the formation of an Ecclesiastical District formed out of the Parish of Bitton. In Hanham, a Late Norman Chapel was restored in 1852. Also in Hanham on Jefferies Hill, Christ Church was built in 1842 which in 1844 became the Parish church of Hanham and the Chapel of Hanham Abbots was made a chapel-of-ease to it.

The rebuilding of St Anne's Oldland involved demolishing the ancient chapel, something for which H.T. Ellacombe later expressed his remorse. This act was indeed a travesty. In the diocesan records of about 1280 there is the earliest reference to Oldland Chapel - 'Bytton cum capella de Oldeland'.

*The demolished Chapel of St. Anne, Oldland Common 1280 – 1829: The Gentleman's Magazine 1830*

The original building had a plain square tower, with a saddle-back roof, which confirms its ancient age. The tower's roofs ran north and south at right-angles to the nave, and the tower housed three bells.

Arthur W. Hill in his Memoir provides some insight into Ellacombe's divided interests in providing additional church places: 'Mr. Ellacombe set out to provide for the proper spiritual welfare of the more outlying portions and at the same time was able to indulge his interest in church building.'

He undertook many changes to the fabric of St Mary's church. The chancel arch was completely remodelled in order to look medieval. He changed the pews of the church from box pews with high backs in which a family would sit face-to-face to pews facing frontwards so that the whole congregation would be facing the alter and the pulpit at the front.

*Illustration: interior St Mary's Bath Central Library/ Bath In Time*

He became a supporter of the Oxford Movement (and his daughter Jane Ellacombe joined E. B. Pusey's sisterhood). He was a friend of the madrigal composer Robert Lucas Pearsall, and introduced chanting into services at Bitton.

Ellacombe was also a keen gardener, corresponding with leading horticulturists and establishing the garden at Bitton vicarage; a catalogue of the trees and shrubs growing there in 1830 was later published, and he had a record of 5000 different plants that he had personally grown with success. The garden was made famous by his son Henry Nicholson Ellacombe, who succeeded him as vicar of Bitton in 1850. He took a great interest in architecture. His 'Parochial Proceedings' are primarily concerned with the changes he made to the vicarage and church.

**Campanology**

Ellacombe's interest in church bellringing led to him being recognized as possibly the first scholarly campanologist. His Practical Remarks on Belfries and Ringers, first published in 1849, drew on his experience of reforming bellringing at Bitton. He invented his ingenious and novel apparatus of chiming hammers that he had introduced to St Mary's in 1822, at the suggestion of a local workman, to enable one person to chime all the bells in the steeple (see chapter on the History of the Ellacombe Chimes). Later, he continued his scholarly contributions to campanology, publishing works on the church bells of Devon (1872), Somerset (1875), and Gloucestershire (1881). Thomas Mozley recalled him as a man who cared 'for everybody and everything', and in whose company one could not be five minutes 'without learning something worth knowing, and in a distinct and positive form' (Mozley, 79).

He was a leading exponent of Belfry Reform and it was largely through his invention, pamphlets and editorship of the Bells and Bell Ringing section of the weekly periodical 'Church Bells and Illustrated Church News' that bell ringers came to be seen as church workers and part of the fabric of the Anglican Church.

**The Compassionate side of Ellacombe**

Ellacombe was in a different sphere from his parishioners. As was usually the case during the nineteenth century, there was a great social divide between the vicar and his parishioners. In Bitton Parish, the large majority of inhabitants were in hatmaking, coal mining and agriculture which gave poorly paid incomes and squalid living conditions that encouraged child labour, sickness and hunger. Ellacombe, by contrast, was affluent, living in a large country house, with servants and in a social sphere of wealthy landowners. There is evidence however that he cared about his parishioners. In his History of Bitton Parish, he wrote

*The Vicarage at Bitton rebuilt by Ellacombe*

> 'Whatever the colliers may have been in former times, it is a pleasure for me to say, that during my long residence amongst them, from 1817 to 1850, they were, with very few exceptions, the cleanest and most industrious parishioners: the majority (for some worked at night) going down the Pits at five a.m. and returning at one p.m., they washed in hot water, on reaching their neat cottages, and then worked as gardeners, tailors, shoe makers, or some other handicraft during the remainder of the day.' (p.222)

The inequality accentuated the separation of the villagers from the middle and upper class of the parish and the associated deference, prejudice and patronization hastened the dissent from the Anglican Church, their embrace of evangelism and the building of their own chapels.

There is much evidence that Ellacombe was very conscientious about his parish duties and very considerate of the needs of his parishioners.

One of his first tasks as curate in 1817 was to bury Benjamin Cains (aged 23) who was executed at Gloucester for burglary. It was the practice in those times for those executed for the body to be given to a physician for medical science. It is not certain what part Ellacombe played in intervening and bringing the body back to Bitton.

Benjamin was part of the notorious Cains family or 'Cock Road Gang' who had terrorised Bitton at the start of the nineteenth century, demanding an annual stipend to avoid being burgled. During Ellacombe's time at Bitton the Cains family were more or less eradicated from the community. The eldest son George was transported for life for housebreaking; Thomas and Benjamin were executed for burglary; Thomas, Joseph and Samuel transported for burglary; James, a grandson of old Benjamin, executed for murder; Francis and Thonuis, grandsons, transported; other descendants transported or executed; three daughters had their respective husbands executed or transported.

It would have been typical of Ellacombe to treat the family with sympathy despite the hatred for the family in the community.

A similar example is where after the Bristol Riots of 1831, Revd Ellacombe went to the Bristol Infirmary to find wounded sufferers. Many of his parishioners were colliers from the nearby coal pits of Kingswood who were pursued into the country by the Dragoons who put down the riot and 'covered the fields and roads with the bodies of the wounded wretches, making a severe example of them.' (Journal of Charles Greville, Clerk of the Privy Council). It seems to have been characteristic of Ellacombe to intervene in contentious situations, demonstrating that what he saw as the right thing to do would in no way be distracted by the norms of the day.

**Clyst St George**
In 1850 he left Bitton to be the vicar at Clyst St George (some 5 miles from the centre of Exeter), succeeding his brother William Rous Ellicombe (d. 1849) as rector of the family living. Here he rebuilt the nave of the church and in 1860 erected a schoolhouse.

He died at Clyst St George on 30 July 1885, aged 95, and was buried at Bitton. In the chancel of the church at Bitton, Ellacombe had erected a mural tablet recording the deaths of his three wives. At the top, his name was also inscribed, leaving a space for the date of his death and his age.

Returning to his Devon roots the small village of about 350 inhabitants gave him time to indulge his interests further. In the twelve years to 1862 not only did he repair the leaking church roof, but he masterminded a full refurbishment of the church building which included extending the nave, reflooring it with Minton tiles, replacing the stained glass, decorating the walls with biblical texts and providing a new pulpit. He was also involved with building the schoolhouse and that of the schoolmaster completed in 1860 and improving and enlarging the rectory. Geology and ornamental stones were a particular interest and his collection of marble specimens was bequeathed to the Royal Albert Memorial Museum in Exeter. His work on the Church Bells of Devon, undertaken between 1864 and 1865 involved him (aged 74+) climbing '452 towers' to examine the bells and their founders' marks. His love of gardening continued, described by a visitor in 1882 as Mr Ellacombe's 'wild garden'. In it his favourite plants mingled with new ones for the visitor noted that even aged 92 'he is not wedded to the past'. Some of the trees that he planted are still with us like the *Wellingtonia gigantica* in the churchyard ceremoniously planted in 1863 by the then Archbishop of Canterbury Charles Longley.

Sadly most of Revd Ellacombe's refurbished church was destroyed by an air raid on 30 August 1940. The tower survived together with the bells but for the remainder only parts of the walls were left standing with the stone memorials shattered. Restoration work began in 1952 with a government grant for 'basic repair' greatly enhanced by gifts and money raised by local people. The building now has a much simpler interior. Two new stained glass windows were commissioned, and an Italian reredos replaced that put up in 1886 in memory of Ellacombe.

War damage and the march of time have eradicated much of Ellacombe's work but there are still touches to be seen of his attention to detail. These include the similar stone finials found on both school and rectory buildings, the bell turrets on each, the lychgate and of course the bells and the apparatus. Never far from a book, two of his inscriptions are still visible carved in stone. On the front wall of the school is carved in Gothic script 'For heaven and for Earth' while on the lintel originally over the rectory front door is carved *'Pax Intrantibus'* - peace to those who enter, good health to those who depart.

*Watercolour: HTE's tomb at St Mary's, Bitton: Bath In Time/Bath Central Library*

**Obituary 1885**

Following Ellacombe's death in August 1885 (aged 95 years) he was particularly mourned by bell ringers. Some 60 performances, including peals and quarter peals were rung on bells across the country in tribute to him; from Edinburgh to Exeter and Great Yarmouth to Chepstow.

The Exeter Daily Gazette reported on his death:

> 'He was always accustomed to ring with his men up to within a few years oi death, and invariably rang out the old year. He was highly practical, and worked his own hand in laying the tiles and in other renovations in his church at Clyst St. George. He was most enthusiastic on all architectural subjects. Within the past two months he had become a little tottering in his walk but was still as clear as ever in his mind, and only recently superintended the introduction of some mural paintings in tiles into the splays of his windows. Deceased was held in high respect wherever he was known, and his death will be a great loss, not only to the parish in which he had so long and faithfully laboured, but also to many in Devonshire with whom he was closely associated in many good works.— Exeter Daily Gazette.'

Bell News of 8th August paid tribute:

> 'In the decease of MR. ELLACOMBE, a prominent man has gone from among us— figuratively speaking, a Prince has fallen in Israel. And this phrase is not one whit out of place. If the deceased gentleman could not be said to be at any time of his life a "distinguished ringer," he was certainly a great man, a prince almost — in matters relating to bells and ringers. His name appeared to be a kind of established symbol which was indicative of an important pursuit of his life. Before ringing literature, in the shape of journalism, had any existence, and when many of those who are now famous in the art were yet unborn, MR. ELLACOMBE was held to be the sole independent authority upon bell

matters. It is our honest belief that many of the so-called scientific notions of recent would-be arbiters upon such subjects did not win his conscientious approval. Others will no doubt, ere long, record their tribute to the goodness of heart of the deceased. Here in this place, where we have the opportunity of giving vent to our own personal convictions, we say that the death of MR. ELLACOMBE is a great loss to the ringing community.'

Bitton is fortunate in having had two celebrated Ellacombes at St Mary's. Canon Henry Nicholson Ellacombe, Henry Thomas' son, was an authority on trees and plants of all kinds. He was very different in character from his father, from whom he took over as vicar in 1850. Canon Ellacombe shared his father's devotion for gardening and continued the development of the vicarage garden which became widely admired and even supplied plants for Kew Gardens. He wrote a number of books on plants and gardening. *The Plant-Lore and Garden Craft of Shakespeare* (1878), written at listed, identified, and commented on every plant mentioned in Shakespeare's works. The extremely successful In a Gloucestershire Garden (1895), modelled on Henry Bright's A Year in a Lancashire Garden, and In My Vicarage Garden and Elsewhere (1902) both originally appeared as a series of articles in The Guardian, the leading Church of England journal at that time.

The elder Ellacombe, Henry Thomas has left a lasting legacy that not only includes his work on church and belfry reform, his furtherance of bell ringing and a definitive history of the parish of Bitton but also a device which has spread throughout the world, bringing great joy in the sound of bells.

**Published Works by Henry Thomas Ellacombe**

Practical Remarks on Belfries and Ringers Bristol, 1850, 4th edit. 1876.
The Bells of the Cathedral Church of S. Peter, Exon
The Bells of the Church London, 1862
History and Antiquities of the Parish of Clyst St. George, Exeter, 1865.
Memoir of the Manor of Bitton, 1867.
Church Bells of Devon, with a List of those in Cornwall and a Supplement, Exeter, 1872.
Church Bells of Somerset, Exeter. 1875.
The Voice of the Church Bells, Exeter, 1875
Church Bells of Gloucestershire, Exeter, 1881.
History and Antiquities of the Parish of Bitton, 2 parts, Exeter,

**Sources:**

A. W. Hill, Henry Nicholson Ellacombe: a memoir (1919)
Oxford Dictionary of National Biography, T. Mozley
Reminiscences, chiefly of Oriel College and the Oxford Movement, 1 (1882), 75–81
Ed. Arthur W. Hill, Henry Nicholson Ellacombe,1822-1916; a memoir
Jeannie Duckworth, Country Life Magazine, The Times, 15 Feb 1916
Elizabeth Parkinson, Clyst St George

# ELLACOMBE CHIMES SUPPORT GROUP

# Ellacombe Chimes Support Website

As the result of several requests to the Goldhanger village history website for copies of music scores in 2015 – 2017, and in recognition that there was no website dedicated to the support for tower bell chiming, it was decided to create a website for this purpose. The material came initially from experiences at St Peter's Goldhanger St. and Mary's Clapham, but as the number of hits increase and more contacts made with enthusiasts, additional information and video links were added.

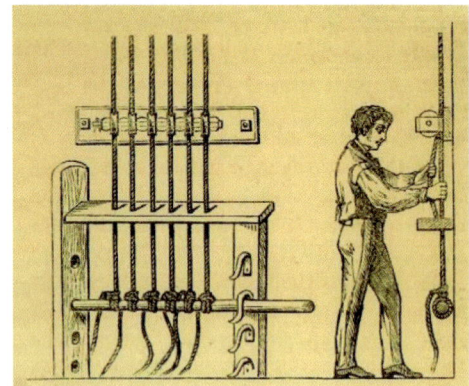

The website embeds the experience of about twelve chimers and has these chapters:

1. Ellacombe Chimes history
2. Identifying towers that chime
3. Comparisons with Full Circle Ringing
4. Why Chime?
5. Types of equipment
6. Alternative methods of chiming
7. Bells out of tune
8. Risks
9. Clapper Chatter
10. Chiming styles
11. Re-commissioning & Preparation
12. Sources of music
13. Call Change sequences
14. Playing techniques
15. Ellacombe Chimes simulator
16. The beginning of a session
17. The end a session
18. Concert Performances
19. YouTube videos
20. Our Aims

The site was originally created in Google Sites with the expectation that by being free, it would have a degree of permanence. However, in 2020 Google declared their intention to replace their website editor and require users to re-create their sites using new editor. This has prompted the authors of this site to create two alternative versions, one being a printable PDF document, if printed on A4 paper it would be 27 pages long.

Google Analytics indicate that since its creation in August 2017, 1,700 users have accessed it in 3,000 sessions. This is not large by internet standards, but in terms of the numbers of Ellacombe Chimes devices known to be in the world, it is high and has justified its creation.

Analytics show that there was a dramatic rise in access to the site at the beginning of the pandemic March 2020, with 1,500 of the total users having accessed it since then. The data also shows there was a second peak in September 2020 when the Ellacombe Chimes Bicentennial celebration plans were first announced, and over half of all users have accessed it since that date.

The two websites are at...

https://sites.google.com/site/ellacombechimes/

http://www.churchside1.plus.com/Ellacombe%20Support.htm

search for:  Ellacombe Chimes Support

PDF versions are at...
https://drive.google.com/file/d/1Z-OPJbB1XpZNucHzXal2AzVHx1UW7eQA

https://e-voice.org.uk/goldhanger-history/files/view/Ellacombe_Chimes_Support.pdf

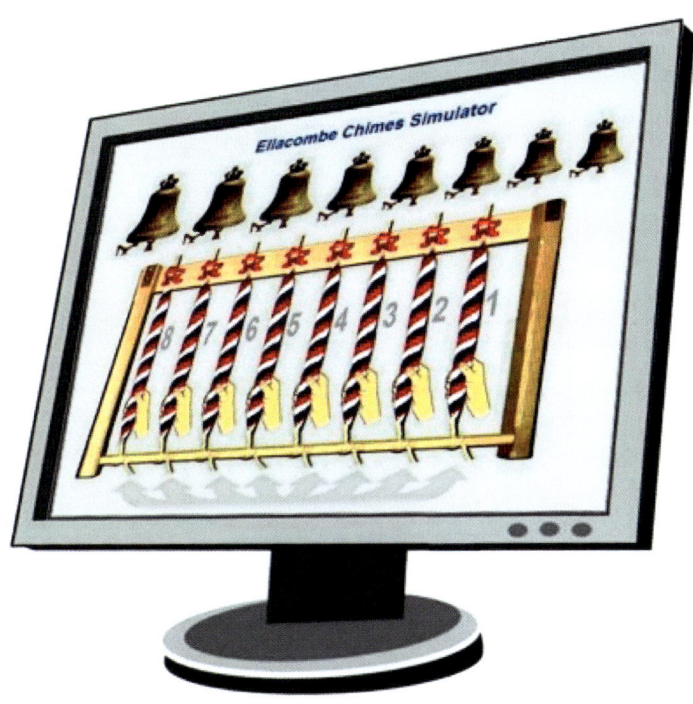

## Further Thoughts

The authors of the Ellacombe Chimes Support site have uncovered much about Ellacombe Chimes and chiming over the five years of the site's development. Even with the experience of both full circle ringing and Ellacombe chiming we have been intrigued to discover so much more...

🔔 The Revd H.T.Ellacombe himself made no mention of playing tunes on his device. He was very knowledgeable about bells and bellringing, writing various books for the benefit of change and method ringing. It seems that playing hymns only became popular in 1889 after the publication of William Haley's book: "The Bell Hymn Book".

The book is a beginner's guide and introduction to playing hymns on the Ellacombe Chimes and he wrote these words in the introduction to the book:

> *The following pages have been compiled, believing that the labour bestowed thereon will tend to supply a long-felt want, and to make the Chimes of the Village or Parish sound their notes in such succession as shall lead, perhaps, to higher thoughts and desires than simple permutation, and changing positions.*

The book has 9 pages of instructions for beginners, followed by the music for 143 hymns using his own style of notation.

🔔 As we have learnt more, our list of towers with chiming mechanisms around the world continues to increae. At the time of going to print it is estimated there are at least 600 Ellacombe devices around the world, with many of those in regular use associated with tubular bells.

🔔 We now recognise that Harrington's Tubular Bells, developed and sold around the world fitted with Ellacombe Chimes from the 1890s on, had a significant impact on the use of Chimes. Several hundred of their systems were installed in

32

churches and public buildings throughout the world and many are still in use, because they were built with metal frames and put much less strain on the tower.

An Ellacombe rack or baton clavier is the only practical way to sound tubular bells, so their chimers acquire more experience than those at towers with both normal bells and other ways to ring them, such as full circle ringing. In North America Ellacombe-style frames are known as "Taut-rope chiming racks" or "taut-rope racks".

🔔 There are many different designs of Ellacombe racks. Having initially been made by local carpenters in early Victorian times then later by several different manufacturers, they come in different sizes and have a variety of rope fixing and tensioning methods. This makes offering general advice on setting up and tensioning ropes etc.more difficult.

There are also several alternative manual chiming techniques in use around the world dictated by the design of the frames and their experiences are equally important in contributing to the pool of know-how and music.

🔔 Many differences between full circle ringing and chiming have been identified. For those who are only familiar with full circle ringing, and for whatever reason, are considering using an Ellacombe Chimes mechanism, the differences are significant and well worth understanding. Twelve differences are identified on the Ellacombe Chimes Support site.

🔔 When presented with the prospect of ringing an Ellacombe Chimes some experienced full circle ringers take it as an opportunity to continue to play the traditional "Methods" they know well. However this is extremely difficult to accomplish from memory and it is very difficult for one person to chime a method fast enough to be recognisable and even Plain Hunt sadly defeats most beginners.

🔔 Ever since the original Big Ben bell was cracked by its external hammer in 1856 there has been controversy within the bellringing community about "clocking" and "Clapper Chatter", but this seems to have receded in recent decades. Clocking was the term used when a rope was tied directly to a clapper. If excessive force was used the bell might crack.

The Revd. Ellacombe wrote of Clocking:

*I believe the mischief is often caused by boys who are allowed to do the sexton's work, and they will often try as heavy a blow they can give, by swinging the clapper beyond all reason and pulling it with all their might. The woeful result is not to be wondered at, for in that way the clapper strikes a more severe blow than it does when legitimate tolling or ringing when the bell is in full swing.*

It is alleged that chatter can lead to cracking. Chatter happens when a striker rests on a vibrating bell, causing a harsh sound. It happens with old style rigid-armed hammers if a chimer keeps pulling the rope after the strike. It doesn't happen with articulated chiming hammers but it does happen with clappers whenever full circle ringing ends and the bells are stood.

Cast metal structures tend to suffer from metal fatigue and may fail after continuous use over a long period. This includes cast iron, aluminium and bronze, and bells are no exception, so you are very unlucky if it happens while you are ringing. Whereas aircraft may catastrophically fail, bronze bells tend to crack but stay in one piece and just exhibit a harsh sound and a different tone. Big Ben Two is the best example, it has been cracked for 160 years and is going strong.

🔔 Before the support website was created there didn't appear to be any form of co-ordination between towers that used Ellacombe Chimes. There is still no standard notation used for recording chimes music but it is probably too late to attempt to introduce one. The most commonly used notations are:
- Plain numbering - usually adopted by experienced call-change ringers
- Plain numbering - with added bars and dashes to indicate music rhythm and timing

- Standard music five line staves - used by those with musical experience
- Standard 5-line staves with addition of bell numbers - suitable for both experiences

To read any of these notations is relatively easy, however creating new music score is much harder. However, all the experienced chimers we have direct contact with are only too happy to share their collection of music scores.

As with many skilled activities, competence and perfection is achieved in various ways, including watching and learning from others, practice and confidence. However with chiming the usual methods have their difficulties. One needs someone locally to watch and learn from, and this isn't practical if the device hasn't been used for some time. The best solution is to watch videos on the internet and study techniques.

Practising as a beginner on the real bells is generally not ideal as it's likely to upset the neighbours who won't know what is happening. They may well be used to the full circle ringing practice nights, but chiming is quite different.

The solution:– use a percussion instrument such as a piano or xylophone to practise call-changes and then simple tunes.

Finally, let us return to the differences between fullcircle ringing and chiming...

Full circle ringing is a grand British tradition that makes a wonderful sound and is undoubtedly not surpassed by any other form of bell ringing. It is a great intellectual challenge and a good sociable team-based activity for many ringers who treat it as a hobby. Long may it continue.

Chiming is very different with many unique benefits: One person can produce a quieter mellow sound that is more appropriate to some occasions. It can be like playing a musical instrument in a public place. Chiming systems are generally simpler and cheaper to maintain, easier to learn the basics, much less strenuous, and have fewer safety hazards, so are more appropriate when members of the public are nearby. Children too young or of too small stature to be taught to ring a bell full-circle can be invited to have a go, and move on to full circle ringing later on. From the point of view of the person chiming and their listeners, the difference between cup shaped and tubular shaped bells is minimal. Only the sound produced is slightly different. Long may all forms of chiming also continue.

These contrasting systems have worked well together for 200 years.
Long may they all continue.

Whatever the original method of construction and the playing mechanism, bells have only ever had one purpose and that is to make a pleasant sound for the benefit of a large audience. If, for whatever reason, they can no longer make that sound they have no purpose.

# The Mythical Dangers of Chiming
## by Mike Shelley

Many ringers with chiming apparatus have come to appreciate being able to continue ringing during the Covid pandemic. In the UK it has been a frustrating time during the periods of lockdown for those with towers that have Ellacombe type chiming frames. For example, at the 75th anniversary of VJ Day, the Central Council advised that ringers could chime a single bell or do a short period of group ringing in compliance with the current guidance at the time. This was disappointing because many towers with bells hung for full-circle ringing also have the potential to have all their bells chimed by one person using 'Ellacombe' frames, baton claviers or other methods. It could be that the disregard for chiming is motivated by a misunderstanding of the possible risks that chiming presents. This chapter tries to unpick these and to allay the fears that full-circle ringing and chiming cannot peacefully co-exist in the same tower.

In the experience of Mike Shelley, the Steeple Keeper at St Mary's (RC) Clapham, London, and co-founder of the Ellacombe Chimes Support Group, the eight bells of St Mary's fell silent from lack of ringers, then a structural report in late 2015 said long-standing cracks needed to be addressed *"…before any consideration is given to recommencing bell-ringing…"* Apparently the tenor and seventh were in essence demolishing the tower. The Central Council only proposed redundancy and disposal, hinting at the Keltek Trust to help with this, a somewhat unacceptable proposal. So, in late 2016 and for less than £9k the derelict Ellacombe frame was modernised and re-rigged with new trigger-action hammers. The result is that the bells are heard regularly, and will be until full-circle ringing restarts. Chiming methods is dauntingly difficult, but Bob Doubles has been chimed from memory, and for "normal" Sundays changes on eight and a selection of minimus methods from crib-sheets.

The second problem after restoring the Ellacombe at St Mary's was how to learn to chime. There was nothing found on the CC website, or from some County Associations. Fortunately, the *"Bells of Warwickshire"* database (warksbells.co.uk), which includes information on many chimes helped and letters to some towers off that list led to 140+ replies from around the country, containing shedloads of advice and good wishes.

And the third problem: *almost everything you think you know about chiming is wrong.*

## The Ellacombe apparatus

Bells don't need an apparatus to chime them, but there are many forms of console or frame, serving anything from single bells to great carillons. Baton-claviers, which are rare in full-circle towers, mostly use wires and cranks to link chimer to hammer, but some have rods instead. The distrust of full-circle ringers is usually aimed at the rope-rigged "Ellacombe" and its modern derivatives, the taut-rope racks which exist in untold numbers around the world.

Ringing before the twentieth century was hard physical labour, and by the mid nineteenth century it was often done by "*coarse, labouring classes*" refreshed with beer. Revd H.T.Ellacombe (1790–1885) was a respected authority on bells and bellringing, so people paid attention when he said that ringers' '*unruliness*', particularly at ringing competitions, was un-godly. In 1820, instead of replacing the beer, he devised his frame to avoid the need for ringers altogether and went on to co-found the Belfry Reform Movement that advanced the evolution of quality bell-ringing generally.

Vast improvements in bell-hanging since then mean most bells are so easily manageable even kids can learn. Yet there are several hundred towers in the UK where people can get interested in bellringing through chiming. At Chorley in Lancashire there are 9–10 students every year.

**The commonly quoted risks**

The received wisdom is that chiming full-circle bells risks damaging them in at least three possible ways: over-sized hammers, clocking and chatter risk. All of these are false dangers when examined closely.

> **"Over-sized hammers"**: Over-sized hammers make sustained frame-chiming impossible. Bells are more likely to be cracked by over-sized clock hammers, such as cracked both "*Big Bens*", and possibly a bell at Hornchurch (readers may know of other examples).
>
> **"Clocking"** bells, by ropes connected to the clappers, is often quoted as a common cause of cracking.
>
> There were some instructive letters about this in *The Ringing World*, the main point being that the real dangers are excessive force (to attempt to make it louder than if it were rung full-circle) and holding the clapper against the bell (more below). Remember that vastly more bells of all sizes are chimed this way worldwide than are rung full-circle. Indeed, it's the Russian tradition up to and including huge bells with enormous clappers. Risk also increases with unusually fast strikes, but how significant is the risk unless other factors are present?
>
> **"Chatter risk"** is when the bell and striker remain in contact and vibrate asynchronously. But it really is merely received wisdom that this is a danger in reality, passed on like Chinese Whispers. A bell cracked by chatter alone is staggeringly rare. Three eighteenth-century bells at Gilling are sometimes wrongly cited, though again readers may know of better examples. But chatter deserves a little more attention.

**Chatter risk**

Articulated *"trigger-action"* hammers are flung at the bell, bouncing away, and so chatter is impossible. Deliberately holding down the rope of an older, cranked-lever hammer after the strike can cause it, so yes, tell people about chatter, but also tell them:

- student chimers learn how it's prevented;
- gravity pulls underslung hammers away after the strike;
- its risk is unquantified because the metallurgical effects of prolonging such misuse take decades to accumulate to a dangerous level unless other factors are present; and, most important of all:
- it happens every time full-circle ringers stand a bell (Apparently, in some towers it can be so bad it's audible).

So, ringers regularly cause 'chatter' but ignore it, then accuse chimers, who don't cause it, of damaging bells by doing it!

**The incorrect use of Ellacombe frames**

The Central Council fears Ellacombe frames being used incorrectly in certain ways (*Manual of Belfry Maintenance*). Firstly by *"pulling the chiming rope too hard"* – this is unlikely for most humans, especially when the length of pull is so restricted; secondly, hammers can be *"set too close to the lip"* – this is improbable, but can be checked by simple visual inspection.

A third reason deserves more attention: The *Manual* says that the chiming hammers not being parked (pulled or slackened off out of the way) before the bells are raised is *"a common cause of damage"*. This implies that negligent full-circle ringers failing to check hammer positions before a raise is common.

Certainly, huge damage can occur if a standing bell is pulled off and hits an un-parked hammer. Prominent notices must demand not only that ringers verify clock and/or chiming hammers are parked before attempting a raise but also that chimers verify bells are down before raising hammers. Everyone must be satisfied that bells and hammers will not conflict before doing anything else, especially when "grabbing" unfamiliar towers.

Chip characteristics indicate the relative movement of hammer and lip at impact. A large "outside-in" chip implies the lip hit the hammer during raising, although conceivably it might have been excessive atypical swing acquired during a particular passage of chiming. "Inside-out" chips are symptomatic of excessive swing while chiming unsecured bells (photo at p.101 of *"Manual of Belfry Maintenance"*). Multiple "inside-out" chips show different swing amplitudes for each incident. This brings us on to 'acquired swing'.

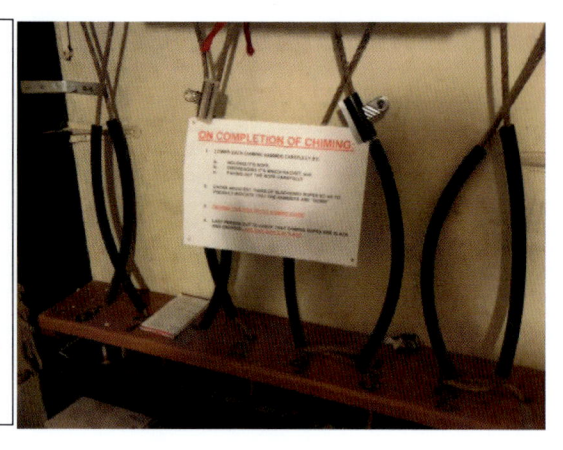

*Visual reference for parked hammers at St.Mary's, Clapham*

**Acquired swing**

Acquired swing during chiming is the only real cause for concern once basic levels of care and attention have removed all the risks above.

Acquired swing is when successive hits of a chiming hammer lead to the bell swinging more and more. The potential risks of acquired swing were unforeseen when the first chiming frames were retro-fitted in full-circle towers, so its dramatic effects were a windfall for the bush-telegraph of disgruntled full-circle ringers. After nearly two centuries it is still imperfectly understood by chimers and is almost unknown to most full-circle ringers.

Every bell's natural swing period is different and, when an unrestrained down bell is chimed, several variables dictate the amplitude of the acquired swing. Chime an unrestrained bell repeatedly in synch with its natural swing and the amplitude increases like a child on a playground swing.

Frame-chimed methods and call-changes can become poorly struck if swing increases too much. Changing the tempo can partly resolve this, but the piece being chimed affects the gaps between strikes on a given bell, introducing another, complicating variable.

Strike marks are an essential diagnostic aid. A clapper swings in the same plane as its bell, so it consistently strikes in the same spots perpendicularly: strike marks on clapper and soundbow match unless there are problems with bush or staple.

But the hammer and clapper swing planes are at an angle, so they strike the soundbow at different points. The first hammer strike is perpendicular to the soundbow. All the strikes on a *fixed*, chiming-only bell will be the same, but an *unrestrained* bell moves after each strike, changing the geometry so the next strike point will be different, and lower down. If the bell has swung nearer the chiming rope the next strike mark is offset towards the side of the pit, and vice versa, so, over time, the hammer mark on an unrestrained bell becomes a crescent. The more swing caused by subsequent strikes, the further the next strike is from the previous, and the further from perpendicular. The further the strike point is displaced the nearer it gets to the lip of the bell and the risk of *lip damage* arises.

**Prevention**

It is unlikely to be necessary with normal levels of use, but if the chimer's repertoire generates too much swing, the problem is easily resolved with temporary *rope stays*. Stretchy polypropylene rope stays from the pit end furthest from the hammer allow bells to move slightly away from the first strikes yet retard them like a soft shock absorber when they swing back through the vertical. If stayed from the hammer end, the bell is almost immobile on first strike and sound quality is degraded.

Where ringing and chiming peacefully co-exist, the rope stay is looped onto the wooden stay above the headstock, but if ringing is to be suspended for a period then the bellropes can be removed and the garter hole used. The removal of rope stays should be included on the Warning Notices.

The diagrams below show where a hammer might hit the soundbow on a stationary bell and one where it starts swinging due to chiming impact:

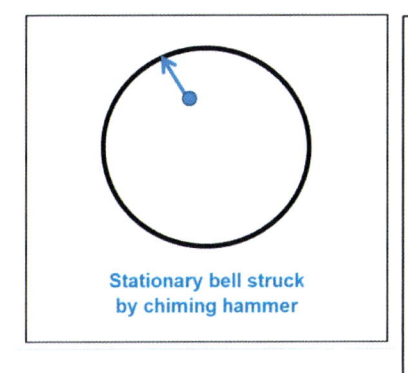

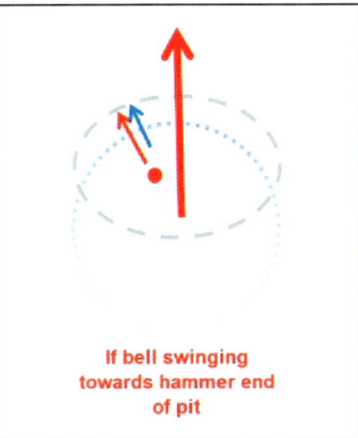

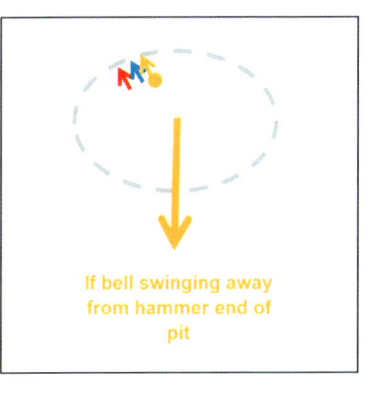

Stationary bell struck by chiming hammer

If bell swinging towards hammer end of pit

If bell swinging away from hammer end of pit

*Worrying mark on unrestrained bell*     *Solution: temporary yellow rope stays*

**The Physics of Swing**

Energy imparted to the bell by the clapper (e), direction of the strike ($v_i$), and delay between subsequent strikes ($d_n$) are constants during full-circle rounds but (e) alters when bells change places during ringing. The bell-rope's movement provides the ringer with visual and tactile references to the amplitude of a bell's swing (A) so the ringer controls it by maintaining or altering her/his inputs to the rope. Ringers also subliminally adjusting their inputs to keep a steady tempo during "clocking" are actually controlling the amplitude of the acquired swing. Ringers swing-chiming, check-chiming or "clocking" unknowingly control the amplitude of swing when they subliminally adjust their inputs to keep a steady tempo.

Bell and hammer may be moving in the same or in opposite directions during frame-chiming, further affecting swing amplitude. Chimers have limited control of (e), unlimited control of ($d_n$) and no visual reference for bell movement, so they can't predict the effects of their next inputs. Fluctuating swing amplitude inhibits accurate control of the tempo of chiming. Each bell's geometry, and each method, call-change sequence and tune chimed has a different propensity for inducing swing, so it is the chimer's repertoire that dictates whether or not swing amplitude will be a potential problem at a particular tower.

**Problems with hammers and clappers**

The geometry of each bell's installation is different and the designed arcs of hammer and clapper may cross during the movement of some bells. They could collide on such a bell if either the swing amplitude rises excessively or if the clapper gets out of sync with the bell.

The hammer might hit its bell's lip or miss it completely at excessive swing amplitudes. Articulated hammers have a ball that should safely fold over out of harm's way. Older, cranked-lever hammers might not fall clear in time, risking lip damage on the bell's return swing. The latter was more frequent in the nineteenth century, and could be the cause of still extant lip damage on many bells.

**Final thoughts**

All steeple-keepers with responsibility for bells hung for full-circle ringing that can also be chimed, or used to be, should, as soon as is practicable, inspect, interpret and record:

　　a.　Chiming strike marks
　　b.　Chips on bell lips
　　c.　The adequacy of clearance between swinging bells & clappers and parked hammers, and
　　d.　Whether or not, and by how much, the clapper and hammer arcs could intersect during chiming.

Risks to bells are far less during chiming than during full circle ringing. It's not chiming that risks damaging bells but the abuses of ignorance, carelessness and neglect. The different uses of tower bells require slightly different ground rules, but all must apply wherever chiming and full-circle ringing are possible in the same tower.

Prejudice against chiming causes towers to fall silent unnecessarily when the nearest full-circle band could provide life-saving support and discover another aspect to bell ringing. The heart of ringing is the sound of the bell, so alternative ways of sounding the same bell are an asset to be savoured and cherished.

# WORLDWIDE PARTICIPANTS
## AUSTRALIA
### CANBERRA
# The Presbyterian Church of St Andrew

The Presbyterian Church of St Andrew Canberra was opened in 1934 and is adjacent to the Australian Parliament House. The Church has a peal of eight bells. The bells are fixed in the church tower and rung using ropes from the clapper of each bell to a consul at the base of the tower. The eight bells, (weighing from 535kg to 89kg and with diameters from 38" to 20"), are rung by two bellringers in the belltower at church level. The peel of eight bells were installed into the belltower of the church in 1968, prior to 1968 recordings of British peals were used.

The bells were gifted to the church "to the Glory of God and in honour of motherhood and in memory of Margaret Rowe" by her son, Roy Rowe. The difficulties she experienced as a single mother in the 1900's led her son Roy to donate the bells in her memory and to honour all mothers. Today Roy's grandson is the Master of the Bells.

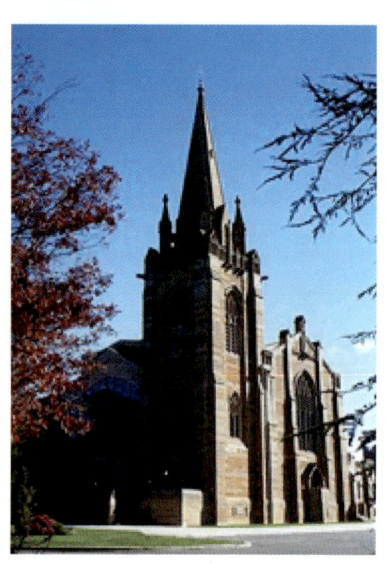

The bells were cast at the Bell Foundry of John Taylor & Co. in Loughborough, England, which also cast the first peal of bells in Canberra at St John's Anglican and the bells of the Canberra Carillion a gift to Canberra from the British Government in Australia's bicentennial year in 1970.

The inaugural ringing of the bells occurred in 1969 to mark the opening of the Commonwealth Parliamentary year. The bells ring out calling people to worship, after weddings, and on special occasions. For twenty-five years the congregation has invited the Canberra public to ring the bells on the 10 evenings prior to Christmas. Being fixed bells hymns, songs and Christmas carols are played. Ringing the bells of St Andrews before Christmas has become a family tradition for hundreds of people throughout Canberra. *Susan Hogan*

# St John's, Canberra

St John's is built on land occupied by the Ngunnawal people for tens of thousands of years before the arrival of British settlers around 1820 who largely displaced the original inhabitants.

In 1840 one of the largest landowners, Robert Campbell, with assistance from the NSW colonial government, agreed to build a small church near his property. Construction was completed in 1845. The church was extended in the 1870s and a tower added.

The area remained predominantly rural until the Commonwealth government decided in 1909 to build the new capital city there. It was named Canberra in 1913. St John's was in the centre of the new national capital and is today a thriving central city parish.

A former Governor-General of Australia, Viscount de L'isle, and his wife Jacqueline regularly worshipped at St John's in the early 1960s until Jacqueline sadly died on 16 November 1962. Lord de L'Isle offered to give St John's a set of eight bells as a memorial to her. The tower was neither large enough nor strong enough to hold eight swinging bells so an Ellacombe Chime was installed in 1964. The bells were cast by John Tayor and Company of Loughborough, the largest weighting 13 hundredweight (660 kilograms) and the smallest 2 hundredweight (102 kilograms). Each bell bears the inscription "J.D.L. twentieth October 1914 to sixteenth November 1962"

Originally it was intended to use the bells for ringing tunes but two of the original ringers devised a way of ringing changes. The changes are written on a canvas chart behind the bell ropes and are usually rung by two people, one ringing the top four bells and the other ringing the lower four. The bells are regularly rung for some Sunday services as well as for weddings and other special church or national occasions, although COVID-19 has led to restricted ringing in 2020 and 2021.

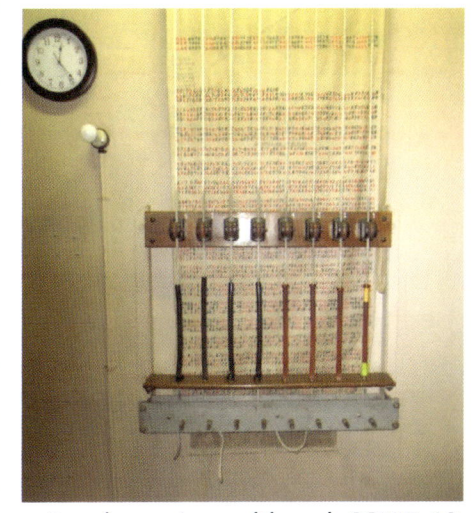

## NEW SOUTH WALES
## Holy Trinity, Dubbo

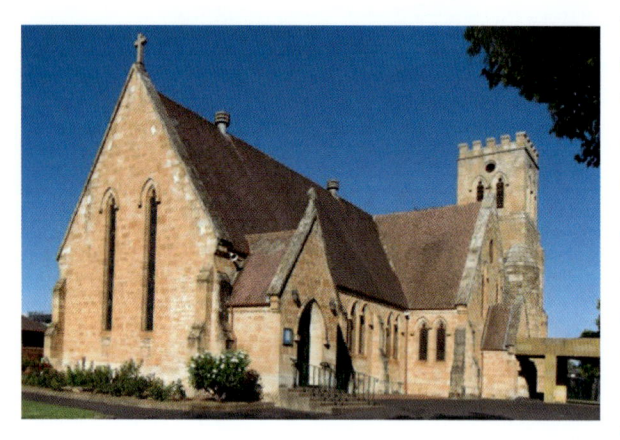

The chimes and belltower, a memorial to those from the parish who served in the Great War 1914-1918, were hallowed by George Merrick Long, Bishop of Bathurst on 17th December 1922.

Consisting of eight tubular bells suspended on a timber frame, the chimes were struck by pulling down on ropes, however, in time the ropes were replaced with steel wire connected to a crude frame, enabling the chimes to be rung by just one person.

In the mid-80s a visitor from England was collating a registry of church and public bells in Australia and asked to inspect the chimes. (At that time, the only chime which was rung was the middle bell rung for church services.) The man climbed the old ladder to the belfry and struck each chime and announced that they were good bells worth preserving.

The chimes frame was in a poor state and had become the home to a large flock of pigeons. Inspired by the visitor and the sound of the chimes Ray Tickle (later to be ordained a Deacon) spent the next two years restoring the mechanism as a labour of love.

The chimes were rung using the keyboard for several years before again reverting to the single middle chime.

Just prior to and during the outbreak of the Covid-19 the Rector in 2020, Archdeacon Brett Watterson "discovered the bells" and rang them during this time. At the end of the lock-down periods in Dubbo Ted Austin took up the ringing each Sunday morning before the 8am service to announce that worship is about to commence.

*Archdeacon Brett Watterson, Reverend Ray Tickle and Ted Austin*

*Ted Austin*

# Saint Carthages Cathedral Lismore

## Bishop Jeremiah Joseph Doyle Memorial Bells

Jeremiah Joseph Doyle was the first permanent Priest in Lismore NSW and its First Bishop.

The Cathedral was opened august 1907 minus the tower. With no plans for bells as yet. On a visit home to Ireland in June 1908 Bishop Doyle Visited the Fountain Head Bell Foundry operated by Mathew O'Byrne in Dublin to order 1 bell. While there he listened to a set of 12 chiming bells being tested. He was so impressed he ordered a duplicate set to be cast.

The tower was built, the bells installed and blessed in front of a crowd estimated at over 10,000 on June 11, 1911.

These bells, 12 in number and weigh 9 tons l2cwt. The tenor bell itself weighs 43cwt Mr. O'Byrne writes under date May 7 1909:

"I have all the bells erected on the framing in the yard. They are the grandest peal of bells I ever made. In fact, there is nothing in Europe to equal them."

The chiming frame is fitted with rollers, brackets and feathered ropes, so that one person can play the 12 bells from a keyboard in a scale of low pitched c major with added f sharp and b flat. For close to a 80 years they were rung with an Ellacombe chiming apparatus but a new baton clavier was installed by Hervey Bagot in the late 1990's , John James Maloney began his role as Bell Ringer in 1980 and is still chiming most Sundays and for all significant events in the church and community.

*John Maloney*

# St John's Church, Darlinghurst, Sydney

St John's Church, Darlinghurst, Sydney has a set of 13 Harrington tubular bells with an Ellacombe chime stand. Back in 1989 when I started working at St John's as Caretaker, I was given a tour of the tower, I was amazed by the size and shape of the bells. 10 years later, I became the ringer and 22 years on, I am still there each Sunday morning for service ringing. I ring various methods and compositions, over 150 hymns and also sets for weddings and funerals.

The bells are a memorial to a previous Church Warden, the plaque reads as follows:

The peal of chimes and the clock in the tower of this church are the offering of many friends and fellow parishioners in memory of - H. Edward A. Allan, Churchwarden of this church for 26 years, member of the Synod of this Diocese and member of the Chapter of St Andrew's Cathedral in this city. He died Nov 8, 1887 aged 55 years. With unwearied zeal and singular devotedness he went about doing good ministering personally and liberally to the sick and needy and labouring actively in the Service of the church in this Parish and Diocese and in the support of all good works. "Well done good and faithful Servant, enter thou into the joy of thy Lord."

*Laurie Alexander*

## QUEENSLAND
## St Andrew's Anglican Church, Lutwyche, Brisbane

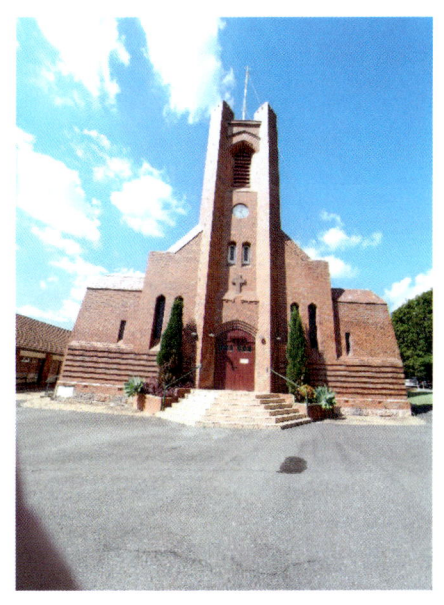

The bells at St Andrew's are situated on land donated by Queensland's founding Supreme Court Judge, Judge Alfred Lutwyche. The bells and its operating system are located within the Arch Deacon Osborne Memorial Tower of the church. The first 8 bells were donated in August 1926 and an additional 5 bells in August 1938. All 13 bells were all founded in Loughborough UK by John Taylor and Co and are operated on tower's first level by a single person at a 13 note hand pulled clavier keyboard that is connected to the bells by wire. St Andrew's had the distinction of being the first clavier operated carillon in Australia

The range of the bells is from middle C to high C and includes sharps that allow the bellringers to play approx. 200 hymns that have been transposed into a ringing language by substituting numbers for musical notes. In addition to the system, an electrical apparatus was made to electronically play the Westminster Chimes. The bells for the Westminster Chimes weighed in all 24cwt 2qrs 14lbs (1250.7kg) with the largest weighing over 6cwt (305kg) and the smallest 1cwt 14lbs (57.1kg).

For many years the bells at Lutwyche were broadcast regularly on national radio on Sundays also for Church services; Easter; Christmas; Weddings and Funerals. The bells have also rung out on Brisbane's Northside on special occasions such as: celebrating VE Day and again on VP day; for the musical tribute celebrating Sri Chinmoy's 15 years of dedicated service to mankind and for the first visit of the Queen to Australia (a radio hook-up to the airport was needed for this.)

Photoed at the keyboard are the oldest and youngest bell ringers, Robbie McKimm (52 year's service) and Rowan Yates (16 years).

Rowan and his brother Hans (23 year's service) are third generation bellringers, their parents, Sheryn and Stephen Yates, both played for over forty years and his grandfather Arthur Bang played for sixty-five years.

*Sheryn Yates*

# WESTERN AUSTRALIA
## All Saints Anglican Church, Collie

All Saints Church is a heritage listed building in the small mining town of Collie in the Southwest of Western Australia. It was built through a generous donation of 2000 pounds from Mrs Nora Octavia Noyes, who attended All Saints Church in Margaret Street, London. Mrs Noyes heard of the struggling churches in the new Diocese of Bunbury, Australia and gave money for an ornate church to be built in the memory of her late husband, Colonel Arthur Walter Noyes. The Church has a mixture of architectural features that include the Romanesque and Byzantine styles. It was built on top of a hill and in the most prominent position in the town of Collie. The Church was consecrated in 1915 and was the first brick church in the area. Although the Bell Tower was on the original plans approved by Mrs Noyes, the tower and tubular bells were not added until 1928.

Mrs Noyes paid the sum of 800 pounds for the 19.8 metre campanile to be added to the Church and Mrs Lillico paid for the 8 tubular bells which first rang on Christmas Day 1928. The bells were dedicated to the memory of Mrs Lillico's late husband, Andrew Lillico. The bells are thought to have been made by Harrington in the United Kingdom and are still being rung today for various services including the Sunday service, weddings and funerals.

All Saints Anglican Church, Collie uses a Clavier mechanism to play the tubular bells rather than the more usual Ellacombe frame. A Clavier is a console of wooden levers more akin to a keyboard. The original Clavier is still in use today and many visitors to the Church enjoy the opportunity to climb the steep, winding bell tower stairs to ring a bell or two.

www.allsaintschurchcollie.org   *Gayle Hall*

# St John's Anglican Church, Albany

St John's Anglican Church, also known as St John the Evangelist Anglican Church, is one of the oldest churches in Western Australia. The first settlement in Western Australia was in 1826, in what is now known as Albany and it didn't take people long before they wanted a church. The people of the town rallied to build it and it was completed to a stage where it could be used in 1844. Through a government grant, it was completed to become the first consecrated church in Western Australia in 1848. At this time, the church would have been able to accommodate the entire population of the town, 170 people.

The church was gifted its magnificent large bell in 1849 however, the community had to wait until 1853 to hear the beautiful tone, when the characteristic tower was completed. The bell was cast by Thomas Meares and Co in London who also cast Big Ben and the bells of Westminster. The bell rings out over the city before each service and during parts of some services. Access to the bell tower, the bell and the flagpole is via a perilous vertical ladder up the wall and through a tiny trapdoor.

The church more recently received another gift, a set of eight tubular bells which came from St Mary's Chapel, Hugh Town in the Isles of Scilly, UK, and were installed in 2009. The bell pulls are in the foyer.

Further gifts, including a fine organ and stunning stained-glass windows, have created a beautiful church which is highly valued throughout the community for its aesthetic, historic, social and cultural heritage. It is surrounded by beautiful gardens, trees and lawns which are a public asset and widely used. The church is a hub of community activities, supporting many important outreach projects. Countless volunteers have maintained the property and grounds over the years. The church, rectory, hall and peppermint trees were listed on the register of the National Trust in 1978.

*Reverend Karen Cave*

# CANADA
## BRITISH COLUMBIA
# Trinity Western University, Langley

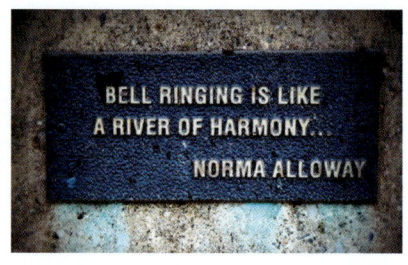

We can't help but hope that the Reverend Henry Ellacombe would approve of the electronic device used to sound the chimes at Trinity Western University in Langley, British Columbia. After all, the story goes that the 19th century cleric grew tired of the unruly gang of bell ringers in his English parish, and so he used some ropes and pullies and created the Ellacombe apparatus to enable one sober soul to do the work of 6 or more strong men. Smaller than his pulpit Bible, the Apollo II bell controller has nearly 100 tunes in its memory and plays the campus chime three times a day, without fail, regardless of the weather.

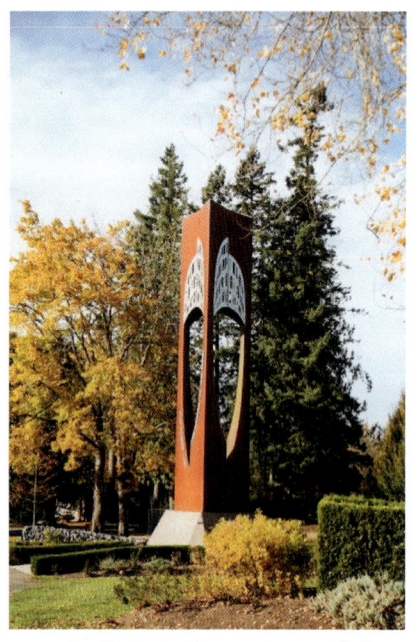

To mark the 200th anniversary of Reverend Ellacombe's device, TWU student Chloe Thiessen was selected to create an arrangement of the tune that bears Ellacombe's name. Just a day after her attending her online graduation service (COVID-19 precluded the usual pomp and circumstance of graduating) Thiessen performed two arrangements on a keyboard connected to the Apollo II controller. Now, her composition and performance are stored digitally; *Ellacombe* has become part of the campus chime playlist and, with the touch of a few buttons at the control panel, electronic circuits trigger the clappers to strike the bells and let the music flow out just as she played it.

TWU's chime stands in a freestanding 15.25 metre campanile adjacent to Norma Marion Alloway Library and holds 15 bells cast by the Netherlands' renown Royal Eijsbouts foundry. Dedicated on March 27, 2000, the chime, tower, and surrounding garden were a gift from the Alloway family in memory of Norma, a writer and handbell ringer. Her words now appear on plaques in the garden including "Bell ringing is a river of harmony;" and "What music lingers in the air because of our journey?" Most prominent, is a third quote that runs around the southwest face of the tower: "YOU SOUND OUT THE WORDS OF THE LORD," which are from Saint Paul's letter to the Thessalonians, not directly from Alloway's pen.

We think Reverend Ellacombe would approve.    *S.C. Brouwer*

# St James' Anglican Church, Vancouver

St. James's bells were rung for the first time on Christmas Eve 1937.

The eight bells, made by Taylor's Foundry in Loughborough, UK, are hung stationary and operated in the tower itself from hand levers enclosed in a frame. But there is also a console, similar to a player piano, fixed in place at the back of the church, and electrically connected to the bells in the tower.

Seated here at the console one may run a pre-cut player roll, or else play from the octave keyboard familiar hymns or improvised tunes, the bells often responding in harmony. Also, there is a rope connected to and descending from the tenor bell into the nave.

This great two-ton bell is sounded at the Eucharistic climax, three times each day at the Angelus, and tolled at funerals. It bears the inscription, "Sound, sound the glorious Gospel to the praise of God, and to the honour of all whose words and deeds have proclaimed it in these parts, 1881-1936." The dates enclose the history of this church while marking the beginning of the bells that continue to sound over this city.

*Paul Stanwood*

# NEWFOUNDLAND AND LABRADOR
## St. Thomas' Church, St. John's

Our church dates to 1836 and is one of the oldest still-surviving wooden churches in eastern Canada still used for worship. We celebrate our 185th anniversary in September.

St. Thomas' was the second Anglican parish established in St. John's, built as a chapel of ease to the existing main parish (now the Cathedral). St. Thomas' was also the home church of the Garrison soldiers stationed in St. John's during the 1830s, and is fondly known as "The Old Garrison Church."

Our chimes were installed circa 1920 as a memorial to those in the parish who paid the supreme sacrifice in World War I. Currently, we have three regular bell ringers whose schedules rotate. The chimes are played mainly in the half hour prior to the chief Sunday service each week, but they have been played at other times as well.

One couple in 2016, being married at St. Thomas', requested the chimes (in particular the hymn "Joyful Joyful We Adore Thee" to the tune of Beethoven's "Ode to Joy") be played before their ceremony. I was the bell ringer who honoured this request.

We also have a big bell in addition to the chimes, which our sexton rings immediately prior to Sunday worship, at funerals, and during Good Friday worship.

Before COVID-19, one of my favourite ministries was showing our chimes to any visitors who came to worship with us on a Sunday. (That ministry will resume once people can travel safely again.) Many of them are used to more modern church buildings and are amazed to hear the chimes and see how they work. My favourite hymn to demonstrate to visitors is "We Love the Place O God" which was written right here in Newfoundland, in the village of Trinity.

*Heather Rose Russell*

## NOVA SCOTIA
## St. John's Anglican Church, Truro

Discussion on installing 10 bells of the best quality and workmanship started in 1905. An offer by Meneely & Co. of West Troy, New York, was accepted with the Rector and Wardens tasked to borrow whatever sum of money would be needed to complete the project. The ladies of the congregation guaranteed at least the interest on any sum which had to be borrowed but in the end contributed much more.

The chime of ten bells was of varying sizes and weights – together, a total of 10,600 pounds. Teams of oxen were donated to haul the bells from the train station to the church.

Scaffolding was then erected such that the bells could be raised up, swung over and dropped onto a support in the tower – a full 20' above the tower's louvred section.

This final location was designed to allow the sound to be let out "fully and freely".

The bell chimes and the set of operational levers below (currently played by our campanologist Cathy Boudreau, pictured) are connected to each other by means of metal rods. The Chime of Bells is in the key of F and it has a wide range in playing capacity. Their sound is described as sweet, musical and mellow-toned.

Peter Allen, the bell ringer at St. John's Anglican Church, Lunenburg, provided some new and updated music in 2001.

Inauguration of the Chimes was held on April 15, 1906.

*Cathy Boudreau*

## ONTARIO
# Christ Church (Anglican), Niagara Falls

Christ Church (Anglican) was built in 1865 and is the only church in Niagara Falls, Ontario, Canada to have a full 10-bell carillon. It was installed in the tower in 1912 and was given by William Lowry Doran in memory of his late wife Alice Edith Doran. The bells were cast by the McShane Bell Foundry Company, Baltimore, Maryland, USA and are each named and inscribed: Love, Faith, Hope, Charity, Truth, Temperance, Chastity, Devotion, Long Suffering and Peace. A new tower was built in 1935 and the bells were re-hung in it.

The Bell Project was begun by the parishioners in 2011 which saw the chime stand renovated, a new chiming system installed allowing the bells to be played manually on the chime stand or automatically by a computerized system and the worn clappers were replaced. The work was done by Meeks, Watson and Company. On June 16, 2012, a public outdoor event "Chime The Bells for 1812" was held to commemorate the Bicentennial of the War of 1812 and the 100th Anniversary of the bells at Christ Church and their re-dedication.

Christ Church has a rich history and the bells have a historical significance in the community. They were rung to celebrate the end of the two World Wars and the Coronation of Queen Elizabeth II who also attended morning service at Christ Church when still Princess with Prince Philip October 14, 1951. The bells still provide comfort and hope to our worshippers as they continue to be played at the beginning of our weekly online Sunday worship services throughout the pandemic. *Kathy Lowe*

## St. George's Memorial Anglican Church, Oshawa

In memory of two founding members of St. George's parish, the Carswell Memorial Chimes were dedicated to the glory of God in 1924. Our fifteen bells were cast by the Whitechapel Bell Foundry, Mears and Stainbank, London, England. Fourteen of the bells are fixed in place, while the largest ("Big Ed", our tenor bell) remains free swinging; it is our call to worship and our tolling bell for funeral memorials. Our bells have a one and one half octave range on the diatonic scale, including four semi-tones. A cabin houses our chime room with clavier, up 56 steps from the main church and below all our bells.

It was estimated in 2004 that our bells had rung out in downtown Oshawa at least 5000 times over the years. Although there is no current estimate, our bells have proclaimed the Good News and brought comfort to many more parishioners and listeners during recent years. Sunday hymns can be heard weekly for half an hour prior to our main Sunday morning service. During the pandemic, when in-person services cannot be held, Sunday morning chiming continues. We provided summer weekday noon hour concerts for many years during summer months. We continue chiming for weddings, funerals, and special parish services. We enjoy participating in special events, including Queen Elizabeth's 90th birthday bells, a tribute of memorial hymns for the late Prince Philip on the day of his funeral, and most recently a Victoria Day concert. Occasionally a guest carillonneur has presented a concert.

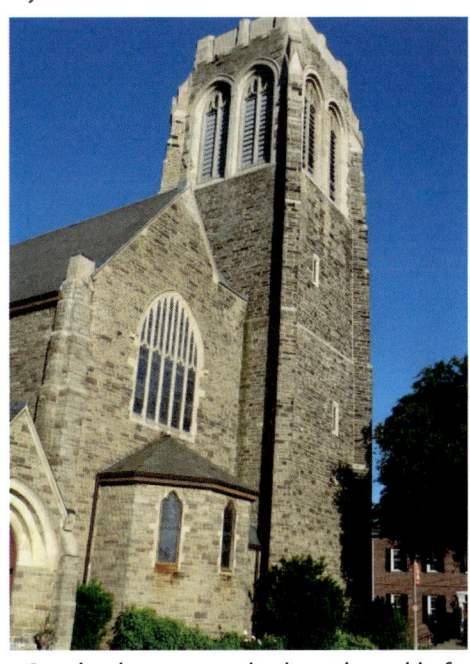

We are the only church in our area with tower bells. We give thanks for the foresight and generosity of previous generations, who provided us with this outreach ministry that touches so many. May our bells keep ringing!

*Deborah Zimmerman*

## St. John the Evangelist, Peterborough

The 15 bell Chime of St. John the Evangelist, Peterborough, Ontario, Canada will participate in the worldwide 200th celebration of Ellacombe's invention on June 26. The outer stone walls of our church were constructed by the pioneer settlers of our community in 1837. They were fortified with buttresses to withhold the walls in 1850. In 1882 the interior was intensively redesigned, a chancel was added at the north end, and a tower at the south end.

In 1911, Taylor Bells of Loughtsborough were commissioned to add a set of 13 bells in the key of C to the tower. It was named "the People's Chime" because it was funded by subscriptions from the entire Peterborough community.

Initially it included both Ellacombe ropes and a keyboard. All but one of the bells were fixed, the remaining large bell could be tolled or played in a static position.

In the 1960's and 1970's two more fixed high F and G bells were added by Taylor Bells. At that time the Ellecombe rope system was dismantled, but the frame remains. Our Guild of "Bell Ringers" will be pleased to be a part of the celebrations on June 26.
*John Earnshaw*

58

## St. Jude's Church, Oakville

The bells of St. Jude's were cast by Mears and Stainbank at the Whitechapel Bell Foundry in 1906. Originally they were to be a set of 8 with only the tenor hung for full circle ringing, and the other 7 to be stationary as an Ellacombe chime. Prior to casting, a flat 2nd was ordered, making it a set of 9, with the tenor in F at 15-1-11. Hymn tunes are rung on a regular basis prior to Sunday services. We also ring rounds and changes, with apologies to true change ringers, at weddings and for several minutes leading up to the start of the Sunday service. One lifelong parishioner referred to these changes as the "hurry bells", meaning if she heard them as she was still on her way walking to church, she had better hurry up!

The church and bell tower were constructed in 1883, with an extension to the nave added in 1955. The tower clock, by J.W. Benson of Ludgate Hill was installed in 1906 along with the Whitechapel bells. The clock keeps excellent time, still being wound once a week, striking the hour on the tenor bell.

Originally the ringing room was accessed by a vertical ladder mounted to the wall with a trap door above. In the 1970's a very narrow steel spiral staircase was installed, making access much easier and safer. Today there are 3 ringers who ensure that the bells are rung on a regular basis. The church is located within a residential neighbourhood in the oldest part of the Town of Oakville. The sound of the bells is much appreciated by not only the parishioners, but by the community at large and we are most grateful to the church committee of 1906 who made it possible for St. Jude's to have such a fine set of bells with the Ellacombe apparatus.

*Dan Tregunno*

## St. Lawrence Anglican, Brockville

In 1837 the first bell was obtained from Scotland with the generous donations from the parishioners. It was almost white, and said to be from a high proportion of silver in its composition. It cracked one cold day. In 1872 the second bell was installed in the tower weighing 2500 lbs. In 1876, on Easter Monday, a third bell was hung replacing the one which lasted less than five years. It weighed 3800 lbs and was cast in Troy, N.Y.

In February 1897, at a special Vestry meeting to plan special observances of the 69th anniversary of the accession of the Queen, the Parish decided on a set of tubular bells for the tower as a memorial to Queen Victoria.

*St Lawrence Anglican Church built 1831*

The death of Queen Victoria on January 22, 1901, was the extra incentive to carry out a plan that had originally been mooted as a tribute to her diamond jubilee, and the peal of tubular bells, from Harrington and Latham in Coventry, England, was ordered at of cost of 1512 pounds. Payment was to come out of a bequest, contributions by the Guild, public subscriptions, and the sale of the present bell, though cracked. A later meeting on March 4th reported that the old bell was so badly cracked that it constituted a menace to safety.

Rev. H.H. Bedford Jones was inducted as the twelfth rector of St. Lawrence Parish on November 27th, 1901. At this same service, the peal of bells brought here by his father's leadership were dedicated and have rung out from the tower their weekly message of hope and aspiration still to this day. Recently composed, In the year of the World Wide Bicentennial Celebration of the inception of the Ellacombe Chimes.

The 13 chimes range from middle C to to E, omitting D# and G#, which handles the range of most hymns.

Information extracted from 'A Tale of a Parish".

*Deanna Lynn Powers*

*Deanna in the Bell Tower*

60

## St Paul's, Hamilton

The original town bell for the city of Hamilton, Ontario hangs to this day above the chapel of St. Paul's Presbyterian Church in downtown Hamilton. New bells were ordered in February 1906 from Meenley & Co., Watervliet, New York. They first rang on Sunday, November 11, 1906. Exactly 112 years later they rang to commemorate the 100th anniversary of the end of the First World War.

The bells were installed in the 180' stone tower by way of a giant rope-and-pulley system which pulled the bells up through a trapdoor in the ceiling of the narthex. Altogether the bells weigh almost 5000 kg, with the largest one weighing as much as a Clydesdale horse.

The first chimer was Mr. W. H. Cumming. The chimes still ring every Sunday when services are held in-person, and our current chimer is Walter Plater, who is approaching his 50th anniversary as chimer.

We are very fortunate that Brandon Moffat is being encouraged to play, ensuring that the bells will ring for many more years.

## Trinity Anglican Church, The "Mountain Chime", Cornwall

Nearly every Sunday morning, for the past 136 years, Trinity Anglican Church's historic "Mountain Chime" has rung out a call to worship in Cornwall, Ontario.

The nine-bell chime, first installed in 1885, was presented to the congregation by Rev. Cannon Jacob Mountain; for many years, Rector Emeritus of the Church of the Good Shepherd, also located in Cornwall.

In the 136 years, there have been a total of 5 Chimers. The present Chimer, Stephen Ellam has been at the clavier since 1984. The bells are operated by a row of nine baton clavier or "pump handles". By pushing down on the handles, one or two at a time, the chimer rings the bells. As the handles must be pushed down about a foot, and in rapid succession, the Chimer's job is a fairly strenuous one.

The bells compose one complete octave in the key of "G" with "F sharp" added. From each handle a wire leads upward to the little room at the top of the tower where the bells are arranged around the four sides of a heavy wooden crib. Hung above the crib is the big bell, which is used in the manner of an ordinary church bell as well as with the chimes.

On the south side of the wooden framework which supports the bells is a small brass plaque bearing the inscription "The Mountain Chimes.". On each of the bells is inscribed the name of the member of the Mountain Family to whom the bell is dedicated. A plate on each bell gives the name of the maker, Henry McShane and Co., Baltimore, Md., and the date 1885. *Steve Ellam*

62

SASKATCHEWAN
# The Anglican Cathedral of St. John The Evangelist, Saskatoon

This beautiful Cathedral, situated beside the South Saskatchewan River in Saskatoon, was constructed in 1912-13, an example of cruciform Gothic Revival architectural style. It replaced a small wooden building built in 1902. Saskatoon then was a new community, growing rapidly with the influx of settlers to Western Canada.

In 1906, a set of tubular chimes, manufactured in England, was donated by a prominent citizen. They rang for the first time for a wedding on February 5, 1907. They were said to be only the second set of tubular chimes, as opposed to bells, in Canada at that time according to a newspaper report. With the construction of the new church, the chimes were moved to the new steeple, which reaches a height of 145 feet.

The chimes, a single octave, are rung from a set of ropes located in the vestry. For many years they were not played due to uncertainty about how well they were attached in the steeple and their inaccessibility. However, with major restoration work underway in the last decade, they were inspected and are in use again. The chimes are often played for the enjoyment of passersby on the downtown riverbank and for significant church and civic occasions. They are connected to a clock and play the Westminster chimes on the quarter hour during daylight hours.

*Derwyn Crozier-Smith*

# Knox-Metropolitan United Church, Regina Saskatchewan

The Darke Memorial Chimes are a result of the grief of family tragedy and the spirit of opportunity in the old west. Francis N. Darke donated twelve bells with an understanding that they would be used for the city and all forms of worship. His intent was likely to restrict it primarily to Christians and perhaps Jews. The spirit was one of universal acceptance which 40 years later was written into Canadian government policy.

For the first 40 years the bells were originally strung in an apparatus like the Chorley configuration. There were one to five individuals playing, the first bell ringer being Norm Urskin, a Roughrider.

In 1967, Lawrence Ritchie, Director of Music, arranged for the bells to be rehung in a circle to facilitate community ringing. He started an apprenticeship program with three interested young teenagers. Ritchie broadened the use of the bells beyond the church boundaries and insisted on a cultural component from bell ringing. As a result, the bell ringers established themselves as a registered cultural corporation.

*Darke Memorial Chimes ready for installation in 1927.*

Since Ritchie's time, most Christian denominations have fed the ranks of the Regina Bell Ringers along with Buddhists and Pagans. On the spiritual side, the bell ringers participate in secular, Hindu, Jewish and other memorials as well as other sacramental landmarks in Canadians spiritual lives. On the secular side, the bell ringer's music catalogue currently consists of approximately 5100 pieces of music from 1250 composers spanning 15 centuries and representing over 90 cultures. The bell ringers have integrated the tower bells in duets with tubas, performance artists and word smiths. They have participated in events like pageants around Royal visits to community celebrations of Fire and Ice including dance ensembles.

The Regina Bell Ringers have handbell choirs, water-chimes and play the Wascana Chimes, another example of the Ellacombe apparatus.

# Wascana Place, Regina Saskatchewan

The Wascana Chimes were originally located in the bell tower of Holy Trinity Church in Milestone, Saskatchewan. The chimes were first dedicated on Easter Sunday, April 4, 1920 as the "War Memorial Bells" in memory of those who volunteered for service in World War I. Upon the disposition of the building, the Parish of the Good Shepherd, Avonlea-Ogema, donated the chimes and the dedication plaque to Regina's Wascana Centre Authority for installation within the southwest tower of Wascana Place. The Wascana Chimes were rededicated April 1, 1987. The pageantry included greetings from His Worship Mayor Larry Schneider and Dr. Lloyd Barber from University of Regina. Wayne Tunison, long-time member of the Regina Bell Ringers, performed the dedication concert.

*Wascana Chimes on the South-west Corner of Wascana Place*

Dr. Thomas Schudel, Professor of Music at the University of Regina, Saskatchewan, was commissioned to compose the *Wascana Chimes Dedication Piece* and the *Wascana Clock Chimes*. When the Chimes are played by computer control, the Chimes ring out every fifteen minutes from 8:00 a.m. to 10:00 p.m. with Dr. Schudel's *Wascana Clock Chimes*.

The Regina Bell Ringers play concerts during the summer months. Each concert featuring well-known music and music written specifically for the Wascana Chimes by the ringers.

*Wascana Chimes Ropes inside the ringing room*

# CHANNEL ISLANDS
## GUERNSEY
# St Michel du Valle

The church of St Michel du Valle in Guernsey (known as the Vale Church) was first recorded in the 11th century, when it was a priory church belongin to the Abbey of Mont St Michel in Normandy. By Elizabethan times it had three bells, cast by the Exeter foundry, but in 1891 these were recast by Warner into a ring of 6, tenor 6¾ cwt, in memory of the son of the Rector.

The bells were hung in a cast-iron frame on the timber beams which had supported the old bells, and provided with an Ellacombe appartus, and a few years later with clock chimes.

The Ellacombe apparatus is not often used these days, because it is housed in the former first-floor ringing chamber, only reachable by a vertical iron ladder up the outside of the church – the ringers moved to the ground floor about 45 years ago.   *John David (Steeplekeeper)*

# GIBRALTAR
## Holy Trinity, Gibraltar

Holy Trinity opened in 1832, built by the British military, following a plan prepared by architect Peter Harrison around 1740, but embellished with arches in a local style. It became a cathedral with the establishment of the Diocese of Gibraltar in 1842.

According to plaques on the wall the eight tubular bells were presented around 1880, by a W.H. Smith (not, as far as we know, the bookseller) in memory of his wife Jane, with the request that on 21st February each year hymn 399 should be played on them. Unfortunately, this practice has ceased, and we do not know now which hymnbook was to be used.

The belfry is on the northwest corner of the building, as can be seen in the photo. Another plaque records that the bells were repaired in 1982 by Bland ship-repairers, Gibraltar. In 2021 the striking mechanism was serviced by a local volunteer, Richard Setter, ensuring that all eight bells sound clearly.

Wires connect the mechanism to an electric control box on the ground floor, made by the clockmakers Smith of Derby. This is programmed to give chimes on the quarter hour during the day. It can also play a number of programmed melodies. A midi keyboard is attached, but only one octave of white notes can be played.

# INDIA
## MAHARASHTRA
# Church of the Holy Name, Pune

Church of the Holy Name, also known as Pavrita Naam Delaya, is a unique church with a clock tower that scales to a height of 130 feet. This church is a gothic-style church of the catholic faith.

Built by the British in the year 1885, the amazing stone design of the tower and the church have braved the test of time.

There are eight fine bells cast by Taylor and Sons from Loughborough, England. Each bell has the Holy Name of Jesus. The tower was begun in August 1893 and was finished in 1898. The clocks were ordered from England but were lost at sea.

Above the clock room, there's a bell chamber which forms a platform above the bells. The tower can be seen from a long distance. From the very start, the church has been in constant use every day. The public services are normally in Marathi language. The Holy Eucharist is celebrated daily in the morning at 6.30 am and this has been continued since the beginning of the Mission.

# IRELAND
## MUNSTER
# St Anne's Church, Shandon Bells & Tower, Shandon, Cork

St Anne's church is noted for its 8 bells, immortalised in the song "The Bells of Shandon" by Francis Sylvester Mahony.

The largest weighs a little over 1.5 tons and was originally cast by Abel Rudhall of Gloucester. To reduce vibration, they were placed in a fixed position. They first rang on 7 December 1752. They have been recast twice: in 1865 and 1906. Today, visitors can climb to the first floor and ring the bells themselves, via an Ellacombe apparatus.

The walls of the building are 2 m (7 ft) thick and the height to the tower is 36.5 m (120 ft). This is extended a further 15 m (50 ft) for the "pepper pot" adornment on the tower.

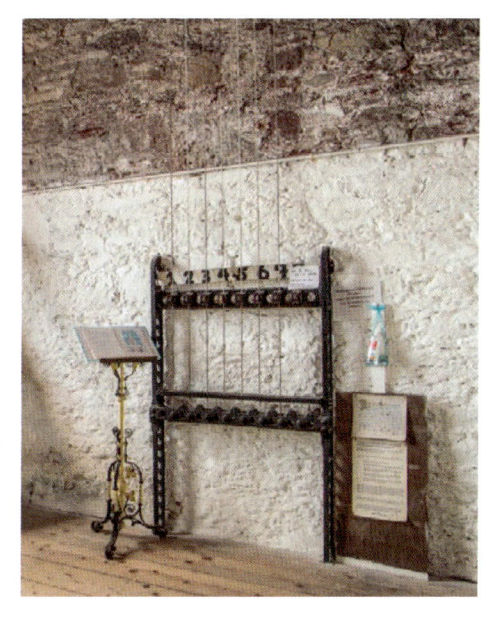

*CC BY-SA 3.0, https://commons.wikimedia.org/w/index.php?curid=81313*

The McOsterich family were involved with the design and erection of this tower and to this day a special privilege is afforded them. Whenever a member of the family marries, anywhere in the world, the bells ring out in their honour.

On top of this pepper pot is a weather vane in the form of a salmon, representing the fishing of the River Lee.

## St Michael and all Angels Church Corkbeg

St Michael and all Angels Church Corkbeg, is located on the outskirts of Whitegate village, close to Ireland's only Oil Refinery. It shares the site with the ruins of an earlier 14th century Church.

The present building was dedicated in 1881, and no expense was spared in its construction. The architect was William Atkins.

About half of the cost was borne by the Penrose Fitzgerald family, who were the main land owners in the area. It is an ornate and beautiful Church, neo-Gothic in style, and contains some fine quality stained glass.

# NEW ZEALAND
## NORTH ISLAND NEW ZEALAND
## St Matthew-in-the-City, Auckland

St Matthew-in-the-City, is a historic Anglican church located in the Central Business District of Auckland, renowned for its neo-Gothic style since its completion in 1905.

As the city expanded, residential and commercial buildings sprung up to the west of Queen Street. To serve the Anglicans amongst the growing population, George Selwyn, New Zealand's first Anglican bishop, acquired land from the Crown in 1843 at the corner of Hobson and Wellesley Street. In 1855 Selwyn appointed the designer of Old St Paul's, Wellington, the Reverend Frederick Thatcher as vicar of the new parish of St Matthew's. On 13 July, 30 people met in the school room to constitute the new parish. In 1896 the parish decided it was time to build the stone church.

The eight bells were cast by John Warner & Sons Ltd at Spitalfields, London for the 1862 International Exhibition, London. In 1906, the bells, in their original oak frame, were re-installed in the tower of St Matthew-in-the-City.

By 1970, much of the original woodwork was in a bad state, fittings were badly worn, and No. 2 bell had been cracked for many years. The bells were dismantled and returned to London for major overhaul. As the Warner Foundry was no longer in existence, restoration work was entrusted to The Whitechapel Bell Foundry. *John Dunn*

*St Matthew-in-the-City's Bellringers, January 2017*

71

## SOUTH ISLAND NEW ZEALAND
## Sacred Heart Basilica, Timaru

Built in 1909 by generous local benefactors and the pennies of humble parishioners the Basilica of the Sacred Heart has been the centre of worship for generations of Roman Catholics in the area.

A wooden chapel was opened on 25th October 1874, and was replaced three years later by a larger church. In 1907 Father Tubman commissioned Dunedin architect, Frank Petre, to draw up plans for a new church.

### Central Dome
At the head of the time is the internal dome, supported by ionic columns. and buttressed by external walls. It rises to a height of 21 metres from the floor. The internal dome is one of the main artistic features, and over this dome rests the coppered cupola (the external dome). The cupola, rises to a height of 35 metres and is in square tower fashion. There is a walk-round base from which, on a clear day, can be seen Mount Cook, and with the aid of binoculars, Temuka and Geraldine.

### The Campanile
The northeast tower houses a peal of a scale of C bell, The 8 bells are each named after the children of the donor Nicholas Quinn. The heaviest, Nicholas, weighs nearly a tonne. They were installed in July 1914. They were cast by the celebrated English firm, John Warner & Sons, at a cost of £1000. They were originally played every hour, until complaints were received from the nurses' home. *Martin Kane*

# St Mathew's, Dunedin

St Matthews Church in Dunedin, New Zealand, has a set of tubular bells (chimes) purchased from Harrington, Latham and Co, of Coventry. Installed in 1906 the bells are one of four sets in New Zealand. Bells range in pitch from middle C to top D, with an F#, Bb and C#, and a tolling bell. Ringing is done from an Ellacombe playing stand that includes a long lectern for sheet music. Over many years, the bellringers have transcribed hymn tunes for playing. Hymns that are tuneful on the bells and have good rhythm are still in use today, together with some more recent song tunes.

Although the bell tubes are stamped with each note, and the notes are stamped into the timber above the playing stand, the custom at St Matthew's is to use numbers in place of letter notation or a musical score. 'Playing by numbers' may seem quaint, but it is easy to teach and learn for non-musicians. It works! A short peel for tubular bells has been added but has strayed from the usual intent of a strict progression to focus on the sound patterns. The peel is available to anyone who requests it.

*The Harrington bell hammers with hardwood hammer faces*

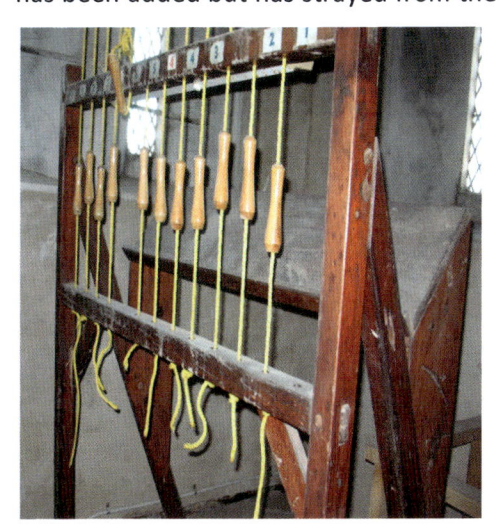

Over 115 years, some of the steelwork of the bell suspension hooks and bolts has rusted badly. They will shortly be replaced with new items so that bellringing can continue. Surface rust on the hammers is being removed, rusted bolts replaced, and the leather retaining straps replaced with a new set. The photographs are pre-restoration. Replacement of the wooden hammerheads will soon be due.

It has been a pleasure and a privilege to learn to play the bells, find what works musically and what does not, and maintain the ringing mechanisms.

*The Ellacombe playing stand and lectern*

The future looks bright.        *Jim Faed*

## All Saints Anglican Church, Nelson

All Saints is a contemporary Anglican church, part of the Anglican Church of Aotearoa, New Zealand & Polynesia.

All Saints Church dates back to 1868. The bell tower was added in the year 1890. The church bells were made by J. Harington's of Fulham Rd, Coventry and were purchased for the cost of 155.00 NZ pounds.

In 2012, All Saints parish celebrated its 150th anniversary. It was planted in this part of the city to reach a growing number of workers in Nelson. Over the years it has established itself as a church for Nelsonians from all walks and customs of life. Alongside local outreach to those on the margins of society, All Saints also has a history of reaching families, children and youth.

Sadly, the church bells at All Saints are not used any more.

# Christ Church Cathedral, Nelson

The Cathedral's eight bells are housed in its 35m tower, sitting on a hill overlooking the main street of Nelson City, Trafalgar Street. The bells commemorate the link between Cathedral and city established by Queen Victoria in 1858 when she established a seat for an Anglican bishop, that at the same time allowed the town of 5000 to become a city. They ring to remind us of the supremacy of God and of the work and worth of the Cathedral in the area since the first Christian service on Church Hill on March 20, 1842.

We have an Ellacombe ringing apparatus situated part way up the tower which still affords a panoramic view of the inner city. There are three bell ringers at present and we ring for three of the five regular Sunday services, as well as for weddings, funerals and special events.

One of our favourite special events is the return of the godwits to Nelson each September when they fly non-stop on their flight from Alaska to New Zealand, the longest flight of any bird. Each September 22, we ring the bells to welcome them home again and to celebrate one of God's amazing creatures. Several of the birds wear satellite tags and amazingly enough can be followed live online as they struggle with winds on their long journey.

The present Cathedral is the third church building on the site and building commenced in 1925 but got delayed with WWII and was not finished until 1967. The bells were donated in 1966 by local businessman and NZ cricketer Sir Jack Newman and his family.

The first church building on the Hill was opened in 1851 and dedicated by Bishop Selwyn, the first Bishop of NZ and originally from Hampstead UK. The second building was needed for extra space and was opened in 1887, being a wooden building like the first. The third and present building is constructed from local marble and granite and reinforced concrete and has a large wooden cross in the Sanctuary that is made from timber from one of the previous churches, most probably that of 1851.

The Cathedral today is well attended over its five Sunday services and daily communion services. In addition, it hosts many civic events, music concerts and public gatherings.   *David Lucas*

# SOUTH AFRICA
## CAPE TOWN
# The Cathedral Church of St George the Martyr, Cape Town

The original Cathedral, demolished in the 1950's, had eight bells, cast in 1834 by the firm Mears and Stainbank of Whitechapel in London. They were rung by "chiming" them, whereby the clappers were pulled by ropes to strike against the lip of the bell. Two very old brass plaques now hanging on the walls in the belltower indicate the existence of an active guild of bellringers in the early 1900's.

When the Cathedral was demolished the bells were kept until a generous bequest by Mrs S.K.M. Smith allowed them to be sent back to London where they were re-cast in 1963 into the "ring" of ten bells that we have today. They arrived back and languished outside the Cathedral where they were hung in a steel frame on the ground and manually chimed with a rope around a clapper flight, until the new belltower was completed in 1979 when they were installed properly. The belltower structure is a combination of new technology and traditional construction techniques, the tower frame being of reinforced concrete with a cladding of Table Mountain Sandstone masonry. For many months the stonemasons plying their ancient craft in a workshop in the carpark were keenly observed by Capetonians, with each stone being individually hand-shaped to fit in its specific position in the wall.

The Ellacombe frame has fallen a little into disrepair but is being repaired in time for the celebration. *Dick Holmes*

### The Bells of The Cathedral Church of St George the Martyr

| Bell Number | Name | Hundredweights | Quarters | Pounds | Note |
|---|---|---|---|---|---|
| Treble | Joy | 5 | 1 | 2 | G |
| 2 | Love | 5 | 1 | 15 | F |
| 3 | Peace | 5 | 3 | 16 | E♭ |
| 4 | Faith | 6 | 1 | 1 | D |
| 5 | Charity | 7 | 1 | 25 | C |
| 6 | Service | 9 | 2 | 3 | B♭ |
| 7 | Patience | 10 | 3 | 5 | A♭ |
| 8 | Sacrifice | 12 | 1 | 16 | G |
| 9 | Redemption | 18 | 2 | 9 | F |
| Tenor | Good Hope | 25 | 0 | 0 | E♭ |

# EASTERN CAPE
## Cathedral of St Michael and St. George, Makhanda

The first ring of bells to be installed in Africa was hung in the cathedral tower in 1879. The bells, an octave cast by John Warner and Sons in London, were supplied complete with fittings and with a frame of English oak.

The frame was not assembled in the way in which Warners had intended. A local clockmaker, modified the frame, placing one bell in a subsidiary frame raised above the other bells. As a result, seven of the eight bells swung in the same direction. This made the bells extremely difficult to ring and it is probable that they were only, initially, swung chimed.

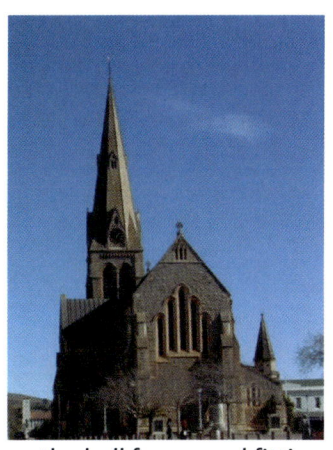

In 1902 remedial work was undertaken on the bell frame and fittings. The bell frame, however, still gave trouble and ringing ceased in 1913.

In 1959 Mr Eardley from Stoke-on-Trent fitted new ropes and undertook sufficient maintenance to enable four bells to be rung. In 1968 a change ringing band was formed under the tuition of Paul Spencer.

In 1993, supported by Rhodes University, the bells were rehung in a new steel frame, donated by H. Oppenheimer, with new headstocks with pits for ten bells.

In 1997 two trebles, cast the previous year in London at the Whitechapel Bell Foundry, were added to the ring. The first peal on the ten was rung on 4 April 1998, in 3 hours 19 minutes: Cambridge Surprise Royal.

Details of the bells are:

| Bell no | 1 | 2 | 3 | 4 | 5 | 6 | 7 | 8 | 9 | 10 |
|---|---|---|---|---|---|---|---|---|---|---|
| Weight (kg) | 288 | 319 | 362 | 376 | 392 | 500 | 698 | 781 | 961 | 1302 |
| Note | G | F | E♭ | D | C | B♭ | A♭ | G | F | E♭ |

# USA
## COLORADO
### St Luke's Episcopal Church, Ft Coffins, Colorado

St Luke's Episcopal Church, Ft Coffins, Colorado is the home of the Mary Lee Townsend Memorial Carillon, a ring of 23 bronze bells, handcast by the Van Bergen Bell Foundry and installed in a free-standing tower on the church grounds in 1967. It is one of three carillons in Colorado, the other two being at the University of Denver and the City and County Building in Denver. St Johns Episcopal Cathedral in Denver only has 10 bells and is classified as a "chime". When the bells were installed at St Luke's, the church was on the edge of town, surrounded by open fields. Wisely, however, 'Van Bergen recommended a lighter tone, but a very lovely resonance in the bells.

Currently the carillon is in need of restoration, new wiring, repair of the bell tower and removal of a large family of bees. Plans were made to start restoration until the serious deterioration of Phelps Opus One, St Luke's treasured pipe organ became an even more immediate need.

St Luke's is fortunate to a have a new Rector who is a bell enthusiast. Her young daughters delight in ringing the stationary Calling Bell stationed just outside the Sanctuary doors on Sunday Mornings, and several parishioners have expressed interest in contributing to a memorial bell restoration. The carillon has a bright future and now that sticker shock from the organ restoration Is wearing off, the Van Bergen Carillon will be welcoming the newly baptized and the peaceful departures at St Luke's for many years down the road.
*Marcia Piermattei*

# ILLINOIS
## Principia College, Elsah

Principia College is a private liberal arts four-year college located in Elsah, Illinois. The picturesque campus is situated high on the bluffs overlooking the Mississippi River and the Missouri countryside; the College chapel is close to the edge of the bluffs with a wide chapel green providing a large quiet area for listening to the Jean L. Rainwater Carillon with 39 Royal Eijsbouts bells.

*Principia College Chapel*

The Rainwater carillon was a gift from the late Jack Rainwater, an alumnus of the college, in honor of his wife, Jean L. Rainwater. Mr. Rainwater also provided for a four-octave practice console in the lower level of the Davis Music Wing of the Davis-Merrick Center for the Performing Arts. In 1999, an endowment fund was established by his estate to ensure funding for carillon maintenance and lessons on the art of carillon.

Both the carillon console and the practice console were designed and manufactured by Meeks, Watson a & Co. in 1998. The current instrument holds 39 bells, cast and installed by Royal Eijsbouts in Asten, The Netherlands (1999). The first major renovation took place in 2017 when all clappers were replaced. The instrument transposes up one full octave and the note range is Bb-C-D-Chrom. D.

*Jean L. Rainwater Carillon*

During the academic year, Carlo van Ulft performs concerts on Thursdays from 11:15 to 11:45 AM and the carillon is played several times per week before chapel services and hymn sings by Dr. Rose Whitmore and college students. Performance lessons are offered by Carlo van Ulft both in-person and remotely. Most recently, Class of 2020 Principia graduate Carson Landry received a 2020-2021 Fulbright fellowship to study carillon in Mechelen, Belgium at the "Jef Denyn" Royal Carillon School.

*Practice Carillon in Davis-Merrick Center for the Performing Arts*

A concert performed by Carlo van Ulft will be held at 10:30am CST on June 26, 2021, accessible at:
https://principia-edu.zoom.us/j/7773231187.

## MICHIGAN
## The Kerrytown Chime Ann Abor

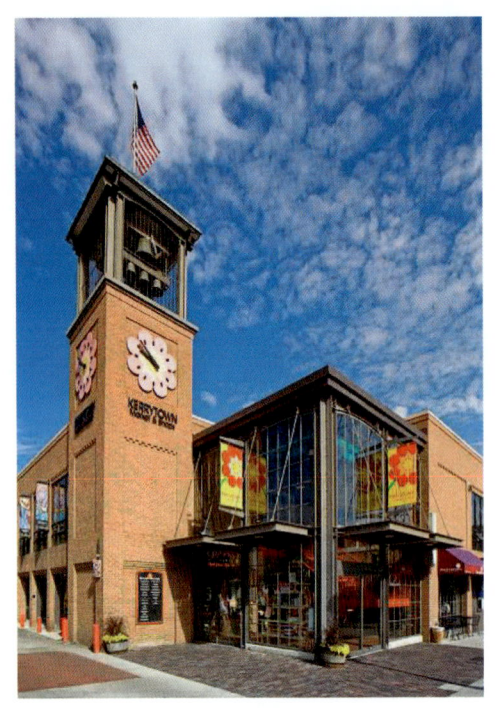

THE STORY OF THE BELLS AT KERRYTOWN

The Kerrytown Chime is a unique feature of Ann Arbor, Michigan. The idea for a bell tower at Kerrytown Market and Shops came from the owners' visit to St. Anne's Church and the Bells of Shandon in Cork, Ireland.

The hunt for bells began. Turned out, a nearby antique shop in Brooklyn, Michigan had salvaged seven bells from St. Stephen's Church in Cohasset, Massachusetts. In 1994, Kerrytown purchased these bells, a C-scale, minus the "B" note.

In 1997, the seven bells were shipped to Royal Eijsbouts Bell Foundry in The Netherlands. Each bell was cleaned and tuned using modern techniques. A new "B" bell was cast plus nine more, to match the original set. Each new bell has an inscription. On the largest bell (700 pounds) it says, "Listen to the bells, telling of joy, sorrow, alarm and the passage of time."

Photo by Paul Bednarski

The bells were shipped back to Ann Arbor, Michigan. In October of 1998, the Kerrytown Chime of 17 bells was ready to play.

The Chime Stand is modelled after Cornell University's chime stand. The keyboard has a row of 17 lever handles connected to cables that pull the clappers inside each bell in the tower. The cables are also connected to 17 foot pedals. Accomplished chime players can play chords up to three notes at a time.

Photo by Heather O'Neal

Visitors are invited to play the Kerrytown Chime on Saturdays at 10:30am and Wednesdays at noon. They can choose from a diverse range of music, over 200 songs, written out by number. Playing the bells at Kerrytown is easy, free and fun for all ages!

# University of Michigan, Michigan

The Charles Baird Carillon, third heaviest in the world, contains 53 bells cast in 1936 by the John Taylor & Co. Bellfoundry in Loughborough, England. The largest bell, which strikes the hour, weights 12 tons, and the smallest bell, $4\frac{1}{2}$ octaves higher, weighs 15 pounds. In 2011, the carillon underwent a complete restoration, returning the original highest two octaves of bells and the original clavier.

Charles Baird, the University of Michigan's first athletic director, donated the carillon. The tower, built with funds donated by many, is named for former U-M president Marion Leroy Burton.

*The 12-ton bourdon bell, "Big Baird"*

The tower and carillon were dedicated in 1936.

In celebration of the University of Michigan's 200th year, the floodlights on Burton Tower have been replaced with a new system that illuminates the tower and its carillon from within, with more than 100 LED bulbs that can be programmed in various colors.

*Jenna Moon (Doctoral candidate in Sacred Music) and Abigail Findley (BA)*

# U.K. ENGLAND
## BATH & NORTH EAST SOMERSET
# Bath Abbey

The existing Ellacombe Chime in Bath Abbey was installed in 1957, replacing an earlier Victorian model. For years, service ringing at the Abbey was only once a month, so an official Abbey Chimer chimed the bells on other weeks. The Chime fell into disrepair in the late 20th century, but was restored by the Friends of Bath Abbey in 2008. It plays on all ten of the Abbey's bells, the back 8 of which date from 1700 (the tenor having been recast in 1869) and the front 2 from 1774.

Since its restoration, the Chime has been in much more frequent use than was ever expected. When public Tower Tours began in 2008, the Tower Tour Guides soon realised that it was an excellent way to demonstrate the bells to the tourists. There are apocryphal reports of Lady Gaga having been played on at least one occasion!

It was during the recent Covid pandemic, however, that the Chime really came into its own. On Easter Sunday 2020, at the very height of the first lockdown, I and fellow Abbey ringer Tom Wareing were given special permission to enter the Abbey and chime Easter hymns over a beautifully quiet Bath. This caused something of a sensation: a video of the chiming that I posted on Facebook went viral, attracting 26,000 views. The next day Tom and I were interviewed about it on BBC Radio Somerset.

*Photo by DAVID ILIFF. License: CC BY-SA 3.0*

Since then, there has been chiming on several occasions including VJ Day (featuring patriotic songs such as "There'll Always Be An England"), Remembrance Sunday (tolling the tenor half-muffled, while chiming bells 1-9 on the tenor's handstroke) and Accession Day (including the National Anthem). Although there are only ten bells in a diatonic scale, a surprising number of hymn tunes are possible.

No doubt Rev Ellacombe would be delighted that his apparatus was of such utility during a global pandemic 200 years after he first invented it!

*Matthew Butler*
*Tower Master (shown in photo)*

# St John the Baptist, Keynsham

If you get the opportunity to climb the 52 steps up to the bell ringing chamber, take the chance. Take care though the steps are steep and narrow, not an easy climb.

On the walls are a variety of framed and unframed pictures and notices. Above the door a picture of Queen Victoria recording the fact that on her death (2nd Feb 1901) a muffled peal of 2000 Grandsire Triple Changes was rung in 2 hours and 7 minutes (without cessation).

Nearby two plaques record long serving ringers; Fred Day died in 1956, a ringer for 52 years and Tom Harris rang for 50 years 1936-1986.

Our Ellacombe chiming frame was installed in 1910 by Llewellins & James of Castle Green in Bristol, who also rehung the bells at that time. It replaced an earlier keyboard-based system designed by George Kingman, a bell ringer at Christ Church, Walcot in Bath, and installed in January 1880. Kingman's first chiming keyboard was installed in 1873 at Christ Church, Walcot and occupied the centre of the Ringing Room, but is now in storage beneath the chancel. It is thought that Kingman's system used the same sort of hammers as Ellacombe's and that the existing hammers date from either 1910 or 1880.

Matthew Higby of Chilcompton restored our Ellacombe Chimes in 2008 and they have been in regular and frequent use since then.

*Martin Pearson*

# St John the Evangelist Roman Catholic Church, Bath

Our church has a total of 9 bells; 8 operated by two Ellacombe Chimes frames and an individual 9th bell operated by swinging. The 3rd, 4th, 5th and 8th bells were cast and hung in 1868 and the 1st, 2nd 6th and 7th in 1878 by John Taylor & Co of Loughborough. The 8th bell is the heaviest weighing 19 cwts 2qrs 24 lbs.

The 1st – 8th bells, in the key of F, are dedicated to various saints, each inscribed "Orate pro nobis" (Pray for us), which accords with the Litany of the Saints, a formal prayer of the Catholic Church:

| |
|---|
| 1st: SS Agnes & Helen |
| 2nd: SS John & Julia |
| 3rd: SS Clement & Valentine |
| 4th: SS James, Aloysius & Norbert |
| 5th: SS Joseph, John the Evangelist & Ester |
| 6th: SS John & Joseph |
| 7th: SS Helen & Elizabeth |
| 8th: Blessed Virgin Mary & St Anne |

There is no record information regarding the 9th bell although we know it is inscribed "Long Live Pius IX, Pope and King". Pius IX was head of the Catholic Church from 1846-1878 (the longest-reigning verifiable pope).

This bell is independently operated by swinging from a single rope at the rear of the church, with the ringer afforded visibility to the Sanctuary and Altar. This 9th bell was traditionally used during Mass at the Elevation of the consecrated bread and wine and at the Blessing at Benediction.

The 1st - 8th bells are operated by two Ellacombe chiming frames located half way up the bell tower, one level below the bells. One frame is normal apparatus and the other is with wood-headed hammers for muffled ringing. Two chimers could work alternately and chime half-muffled if desired.

Sources: Keltek Trust, St John the Evangelist Parish Archive.

*Michael Gibbens*

BRISTOL
# Church of The Holy Nativity, Knowle

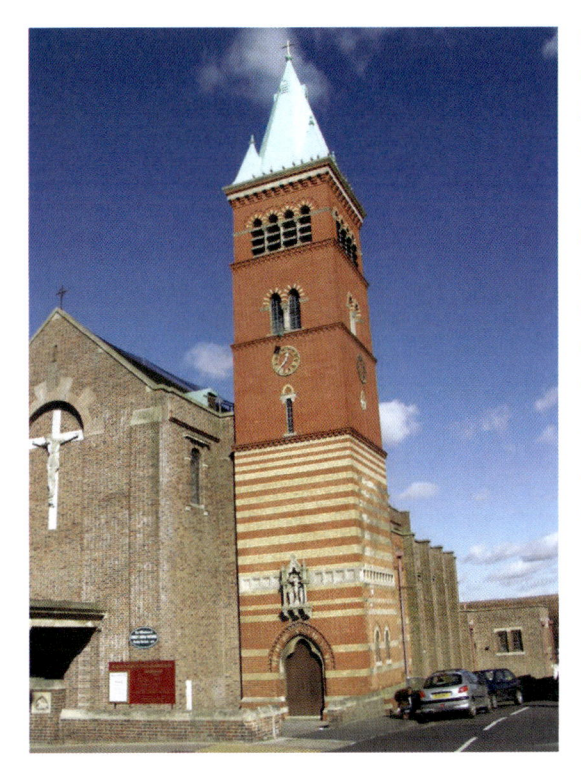

In 1932 the Tower, Clock and a peal of eight bells, cast and installed on two levels by Gillett & Johnston, in the Key of G was added to the church, and is now very much a local landmark.

Unfortunately, during the first heavy air raid on Bristol in November 1940 the church was destroyed but the tower survived. For the following eighteen years the Parochial Hall was used for worship until the new church was completed.

The Ellacombe Chimes have proved very useful over the years as bellringers are only here once a month.

Particularly during the pandemic, with the opening up of churches for worship I have been able to chime for the Sunday Service, whether it is rounds and call changes or hymns and tunes including the supporters songs for the two Bristol football teams.

I have recently been given a book of tunes which can be played on the chimes, including general hymns, Christmas and Easter, nursery rhymes and popular tunes.

*Trevor King, Tower Captain*

## CAMBRIDGESHIRE
## All Saints, St Ives

On 25 September 1930 the Bishop of Ely dedicated eight new bells for All Saints, St Ives, together with a new Ellacombe chiming apparatus. This was the final act of a story that began dramatically 12 years earlier on 23 March 1918, when an aeroplane of the Royal Flying Corps collided with the church spire, killing the pilot, 2nd Lt Kenneth Wastell, demolishing the top of the spire, causing severe damage to the church and silencing the bells.

There has been a church at St Ives on the banks of the Great Ouse since 971. It was rebuilt around 1150, and again from 1470. The bells are first mentioned in 1559, and a new ring of 8 was cast in 1723. The spire was rebuilt after its destruction by a great storm in 1741, and again in 1879. After the plane crash of 1918 restoration of the tower and spire was completed in 1924 and then the parishioners started to raise yet more money for the bells. This took another five years, the invoice from Whitechapel foundry to the vicar (the Revd Oscar Wilde, cousin of the notorious playwright) is dated 8 February 1930 and includes "providing an Ellacombe Chiming apparatus for the eight bells". The bells are now rung from the church floor, with the bell frame in what had until 1918 been the ringing room, and the Chimes are in that bell chamber, just below the bells themselves. This means that the Apparatus is not easily accessible or even visible.

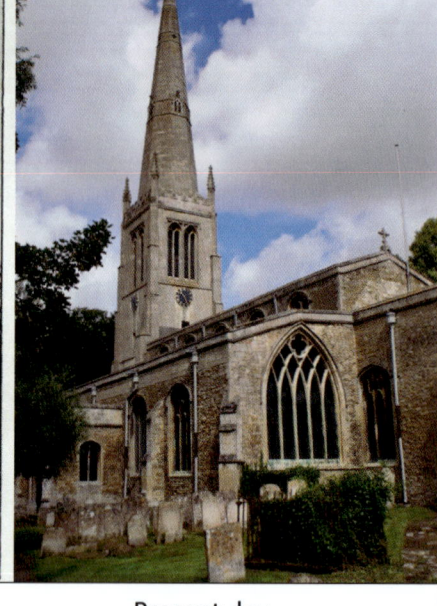

Damage by aeroplane in 1918

Present day

Although the church now has a strong band of ringers, the chimes are also used frequently. At Christmas, carol services are regularly preceded by chimed carols rather than full-circle ringing, and over the last 12 months when it has not been possible to ring normally, chiming has proved a good alternative on a number of occasions, on Sundays and for the occasional wedding. *Simon Kershaw*

# St Margaret's Hemingford Abbots

The Ellacombe Chime apparatus has always been used at St Margaret's church but never more so than during the Covid pandemic of 2020-21 when all tower bell ringing ceased. It is likely that the mechanism was installed in 1894 when the bells were re-hung although it may have been later in 1923 when repairs were made to the bells.

Over the following years it fell into disrepair and it was not until 1994, when the bells were again re-hung with new bearings and the clappers refurbished, that it was decided to resuscitate the apparatus once more.

The chimes have been invaluable during the pandemic lockdowns as this was the only safe way to ring. When the church building was allowed to reopen for private prayer the bells were chimed twice a week. With the resumption of in-person services chiming called people to church. The villagers have been very appreciative of both our tower bell ringing and especially of the chiming during the recent difficult times. When the bells are not rung locals query why!

One Sunday afternoon our most experienced Ellacombe chimer was leaving the church when he met a couple from the neighbouring village who asked where the recording was taken from! We now have over 100 tunes many of which have been adapted especially for the 6 bells. Chiming sessions usually commence with a little 'made up' tune often followed by 'The Bells of St. Marys'.

During the initial lockdown, war-time tunes such as 'We'll Meet Again' were chimed as part of the end of World War 2 celebrations. In remembrance of the Duke of Edinburgh tunes such as 'Should All Acquaintance Be Forgot' were chimed. Favourite songs of church members have also been adapted for chiming and of course carols are always rung at Christmas Time.

*Sharon Williams, Tower Captain*

## COUNTY DURHAM
## Our Lady Immaculate and St. Cuthbert's R.C. Church, Crook

The Catholic Church in Crook was built in 1853 to the design of Edwin Pugin. It was intended to have a tower and spire, funds meant this was never completed. 44 Years later parish priest Augustine Pippet from Somerset, having paid off all debts, decided to complete the new 90 feet tower with Clock and Chimes in celebration of the Diamond Jubilee of Queen Victoria's reign in 1897. A Bazaar was held to raise money with the help of the townspeople of Crook. A new design was drawn up. John Potts of Leeds provided the clock, while John Warner and Sons of Cripplegate, London provided the Peal of 8 bells and Ellacombe Chime Rack.

Each bell is dedicated to a saint or saints. 7 bells are in a permanent fixed position whilst the 8th and largest bell dedicated to Saint Cuthbert can be swung. We avoid full circle ringing of this bell as it is known to rock the tower. The bells have been played very little over the years until 1993, following a demonstration, a then 12-year-old Aaron Cowen was shown the ropes and has played them ever since. We have yet to find someone willing to take on the task for the future. In 1997 the tower celebrated its 100th anniversary and bells were played throughout, playing popular hymns from 1897 along with some local tunes such as the Blaydon Races. Princess Diana had also passed and so even Elton John's Candle in the Wind featured among them. In 2011 the Duke of Kent visited to open new facilities (the St. Cuthberts Centre) for the parish and the bells were chimed playing "Jerusalem" and "I Vow to thee my Country".   *Aaron Cowen*

88

# DERBYSHIRE
## St Matthew's Church, Hayfield

There has been a Church in Hayfield in its present location since 1386. In 1793 the Church tower was added and six bells installed. The rest of the Church was rebuilt in 1818, and the tower raised in 1894 to accommodate a new clock with 4 faces.

The original 6 bells were found to be in a dangerous condition in about 1906/7. Money was raised locally to overhaul them of which £250.00 was used in improvements to the belfry including "the provision of arrangements for the addition of 2 other bells at some future date to make a full peal of 8, and the addition of the chimes." (The Advertiser June 25th, 1909). Sarah Wilkes who died in 1919 left money in her will for the 2 new bells, which were cast in 1946 at Taylor's Foundry. There are no exact records as to when the Ellacombe Chime was installed, but it appears to have been in about 1909 when the overhaul of the bells was carried out. It was presumably modified later to operate on all 8 bells.

It is understood that the Chimes were used quite regularly from the 1970's to 1980's by Mr Norman Duckett, who also looked after the clock. He rang hymn tunes and Carols, copies of which were found in the tower. The Chimes have not been used since then and the ropes on the frame were disconnected in about 2000.

After the first National Lockdown due to the Covid 19 pandemic in 2020 the current tower captain (Reg Radford) and his wife (Elaine) decided to try and restore the Chimes. This was achieved in time for the Christmas services. Services ceased during the third national lockdown in January 2021. Once they resumed the Chimes have been used prior to the Sunday morning services.

*Elaine Radford*

89

# St. James, Riddings

Riddings is a village in Derbyshire, a few miles south of Alfreton.

The bells are a chime of ten tubular bells by Harrington & Latham of Coventry. They are the only ring of ten Harrington's tubular bells in Derbyshire. In the early 2000's they were found to be in a very poor condition, so bad that there was a fear one of the bells could actually fall from the tower, seeing as they are hung over the entrance to the church, this was more than slightly concerning!

The choice had to be made whether to restore the bells, or scrap them. Happily, the PCC agreed to restore them and villagers raised over £7000 for this work. Nicholson Engineering Ltd of Dorset completed the rehang and restoration in early 2008, with assistance from local labour.

The bells range in length from 50 inches to 90 inches, and are estimated to weigh from 25kg (half a hundred weight) up to 75kg (one and a half hundred weight).

The date of their installation is not known, but, from their style, they are thought to date from around 1900. The majority of fixtures and fittings were replaced, however, the bells are still original, but have been cleaned up and tuned. They are now in the key of C. The bells are rung by means of ropes hanging in a wooden frame. Similar to an Ellacombe apparatus. Each rope is then pulled to strike the hammer against the bell. Using this method, it is possible for one person to chime all ten bells.

*Anne Westman*

# DEVON
## St Michael and All Angels, Heavitree, Exeter

The church of St Michael and All Angels, Heavitree (part of the city of Exeter) was built in 1897. An earlier tower had been constructed from the soft, local sandstone and therefore was not robust enough to support the weight of a peal of bells. The tall and elegant granite tower that is seen today was therefore specifically designed to house the eight bells with a tenor weighing 26cwt that are widely regarded as some of the finest work ever to come from the Loughborough bell foundry of John Taylor & Co, and they remain a great favourite with visitors and local ringers alike.

It is therefore thought that the Ellacombe chimes were installed at the same time. From the hammers that strike the bells high up in the tower, the ropes drop down to the apparatus situated in the porch, just inside the entrance door to the church on the west face of the tower.

The frame that the ropes are attached to is a simple wooden construction with no plaques or labels to indicate who the manufacturer might be, and a tongued-and-grooved wooden door keeps everything tidily hidden away. The chiming ropes then pass through the ringing chamber upstairs, where a hook-and-eye system connects or disconnects the hammers, depending on whether the bells are to be rung by the ringers, or chimed from the porch.

*Wendy Campbell*

# St Margaret's, Topsham

St Margaret's church, Topsham, is situated a few miles south of Exeter and stands overlooking the River Exe. The church building was rebuilt over the period 1874-6 but the medieval tower, which houses the six bells, dates from the mid-fifteenth century. Initially, the cost of rebuilding the church did not extend to the tower or the refurbishment of the bells, save for the installation of the Ellacombe chimes in 1875.

According to the Devon and Exeter Gazette in 1911, 'the chiming apparatus, which has been used since 1875, was erected under the Rev. H. T. Ellacombe's supervision, and in accordance with his patent.' Henry Thomas Ellacombe was at this time the vicar at nearby Clyst St George and was very involved in bell ringing in the area, having been instrumental in setting up the Guild of Devonshire Ringers the previous year in 1874.

The chimes were the sole method of ringing the bells between 1875 and 1912 due to the belief that one of the bells was cracked. This was found not to be the case when they were given a significant overhaul in 1911/12. Topsham joined the Guild at this time and has maintained a strong tradition of bell ringing ever since. Notably, the bells were rung by a band of local women during the first world war to keep them sounding and this is commemorated by a plaque in the tower.

The chimes were refurbished by one of Topsham's ringers in 2015 and they are used regularly by the non-ringing church members as a safe means to toll the tenor for the early service on a Sunday morning. They are used by the ringers to play tunes on occasion and are ideal for enabling visitors to ring the bells, especially those who may not be able to manage the ropes. *Matt Pym, Tower Captain*

# St David's Church, Exeter

The present Caröe church is the fourth church on or near the site and was consecrated on 9th January 1900. The bells are from the previous "Pepper-pot church" consecrated in 1817 and built in the classical style with a circular tower, hence the nickname. The middle six bells date from 1817, a new treble and tenor were added in 1889 to mark Queen Victoria's Golden Jubilee in 1887. In 1897 the "Pepper-pot church" was demolished and the present church built within its footprint.

The bell frame and gear are by Stokes of Woodbury and dated 1899. The bells were overhauled in 1973. The Ellacombe Chiming gear was retained and restrung by a radio ham using synthetic rope that he used for staying his aerials; hard wearing but rough on the hands! The bells are chimed from a frame in the ringing chamber. There are holes in the floor leading to the muniments' room below but there is no evidence of a frame ever having been fitted there. The tenor rope goes on down to the Lady Chapel from where it can be chimed, mostly as a Sanctus bell. Slightly unusually, our chimes are arranged, 1 to 8, from left to right.

Ringer numbers have fluctuated over the years and the Ellacombe Chimes have been periodically brought into service. When Tony Crabtree left, in the 1980s, he gave us a copy of his book, *"Music for Handbells and Church Bells"*. We still play hymns and carols from it and it is well thumbed!

Since 1990 St David's has been the Exeter University Guild of Ringers home tower, very appropriate as the university is in the parish. Ringer numbers have increased but there can sometimes be shortages at holiday times.

During the Pandemic the chimes have been in use in order to maintain social distancing regulations. Over the years the Ellacombe Chimes have proved themselves to be a valuable asset.

*Geoff Crockett*

## St. Mary's, Offwell

St. Mary's is best known for the Copleston family who provided a continuous succession of Rectors from 1772 until 1953, including the distinguished Edward Copleston, Bishop of Llandaff, whose eccentric Bishop's Tower is just one of many architectural legacies in Offwell.

Around the time that Rev. Ellacombe was having problems with his own 'unruly and drunken ringers' the Rector at St. Mary's, John Gaius Copleston, was trying, unsuccessfully, to dissuade his ringers from celebrating Guy Fawkes night and ringing in the New Year instead.

Photo courtesy Melanie Jolly

During June 2021 St. Mary's held an exhibition celebrating the history of bell ringing at Offwell and the renovation of the Ellacombe Chimes.

Our present Bell Captain, John Tristram, is 80 years of age and during the Covid-19 lockdowns John was shielding but he was able to do some work in the tower that he had in mind to do for some considerable time, including repairing the Ellacombe Chimes.

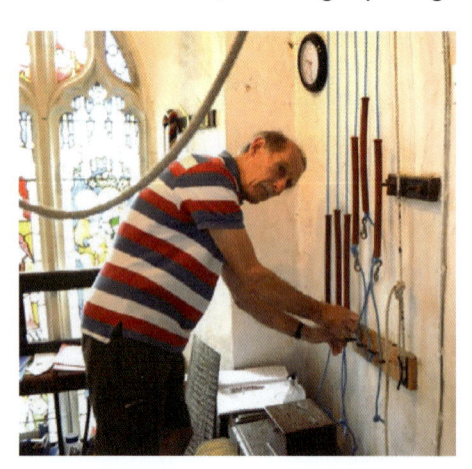

"John Seymour, the previous Bell Captain, told me that when he first came to Offwell the Rector would sometimes play tunes on the chimes, but when I became Tower Captain I found that several of the pulleys which brought ropes down to the chime frame in the ringing chamber were jammed. The ropes themselves were unserviceable. Some were actually parted, others knotted together, all worn and frayed. After the first lockdown Cllr. Clive Whithear very kindly helped me bring the mechanism into working condition and on Christmas morning (2020) I was able to chime the bells to welcome parishioners to morning service.

I found that tension of the control ropes is very critical. The ropes operate a hammer inside the bell as it hangs down; too vigorous a strike swings the bell so much that it's not in position for the next strike. I need to do some fine tuning for the Ellacombe 200- year-anniversary on 26th June."

*John Tristram*

## Church of St George, Clyst St George

With a renowned campanologist as an earlier rector the history of the church bells has been well documented. In his book on The Church Bells of Devon Ellacombe wrote that the tower had three old bells. The oldest (now the fifth bell), was originally cast in an Exeter foundry about 1595 by John Bydran. It bore the wording 'Embrace trew museck'. Ellacombe added three new bells, a tenor and two trebles between 1860 and 1864. The first treble was a memorial to Prince Albert paid for by subscription. The tone of the tenor bell was not considered by Ellacombe to be full enough so he had it recast in 1864 in memory of his grandson who died that year aged 10 years.

Worse was to come for the church was hit by an incendiary bomb in August 1940 causing the bells to crack and become heat crazed so all were recast by Mears and Stainbank at the Whitechapel Foundry in London in 1953 and dedicated later that year. These new bells were all given the inscriptions of their predecessors except for the recast 5th bell whose inscription band is displayed in the tower. All the bells bear a crown and royal cypher E II R to commemorate the coronation held that year.

Ellacombe probably installed the original chiming apparatus in the 1860's when the bells were rehung so allowing a sole ringer to chime all six bells. As a result of the war damage we now have a replacement set erected in the tower. The bells are rung for Sunday services by a group of ringers from several local churches. We also have a very loyal bell ringer who rings the chimes.

An eight-day clock was put in the tower in 1861 with a striking movement to arrange a blow every half hour. Ellacombe described the movements as 'peculiar to itself'! After the war a new clock was installed striking on the hour on the tenor bell as it does now.  *Elizabeth Parkinson*

John Langabeer chiming the apparatus on 10 May 2021

## St Michael the Archangel, Chagford

The current ring of 8 (18-0-22) at St Michael the Archangel, Chagford, Devon, was being recast in 1914 by Taylor's when the Great War broke out, and an inscription to that effect was included on the Tenor. They were hung on elm head stocks in a new oak frame by local bellhanger, William Aggett & Sons, and Ellacombe chiming apparatus fitted. The bells were Simpson-tuned after casting, and although are said to be in the key of E, the frequencies put them somewhere between concert pitch E & F. In 2017, the bells were rehung on cast iron headstocks in a metal frame; no further tuning was required. The Ellacombe chiming apparatus was reinstalled by Andrew Mills of Taylor's with trigger action hammers.

The chimes were sometimes used by Percy Rice, Tower Captain 1946-76, to play hymns before Evensong when there was an insufficient number of ringers. His old cards are still attached to the inside of the chime cupboard door.

It was during the Covid 19 Pandemic that the chimes really came into their own, and through the dedication of Tower Captain, Jon Bint, enabled bells to be heard every Sunday right throughout at such times when ringing was not permitted. The range of tunes performed would likely have caused Rev'd Ellacombe some consternation, including as it did: 'Frère Jacques' (in cannon!) at the start of BST, 'Somewhere Over the Rainbow,' and 'Lean On Me', during 'Clap for Carers', 'Jerusalem' on St George's day, 'The Dambusters' March' on the VE Day Anniversary, and a selection of Elvis love songs for St Valentine's Day 2021! The widespread appreciation within the local community of all the chiming was evident by the very many Facebook postings at the time on Chagford Hub.   *Jon Bint*

# St Giles' Church, Kilmington

According to the church inventory of 1534 there were four bells in the tower and by 1895 these had been replaced, augmented eventually to six bells and a ringing chamber floor had been constructed.

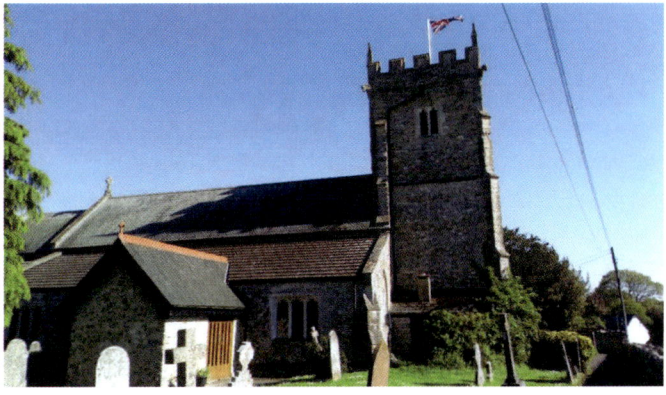

The Ellacombe Chiming system stands alongside a set of six handbells that were provided for the new ringing chamber in 1895 and we believe this was when the Ellacombe Chimes arrived.

They are still there today and in recent years have only been used to play some Christmas music prior to the various December services. However, during the Coronavirus Pandemic 2020/21 Kilmington residents have been delighted to hear the bells chiming on many occasions for services, weddings, and funerals.

How lucky we are that they were not removed years ago!

# DORSET
## St Andrew's, West Stafford

St Andrew's Church has been a place of worship for over 700 years; the first Rector was appointed in 1307.

The tower, affiliated to the Salisbury Diocesan Guild of Ringers (SDGR), has 3 bells which were cast by John Wallis in Salisbury. The treble and tenor are dated 1620 and the middle bell dated 1595. None of the bells has ever been tuned but they are considered "a bright and cheerful little ring". In diameter they are 28", 30" & 33".

They are reputed to be "the three bells of Talbotheys" in Thomas Hardy's novel 'Tess of the D'Urbervilles'.

The Ellacombe Frame has, quite literally, been a Godsend during the Coronavirus pandemic when no bells were allowed to be rung in the traditional manner. When Services were permitted we could use the frame to chime the bells; an anonymous quote - "bells are the external choir that calls out across space & time".

This is a Ground Floor Ring with the ropes sited in the tiny vestry of this very small church - due to the mandatory Covid Risk Assessment only one person at a time was allowed in there!

The church has a couple of interesting stained-glass windows - the Devil Window and the Angel Window. There are only a few Devil Windows in Europe - ours is a striking depiction with the figure itself in scarlet red with black wings. The Angel Window is unusual because it is a rare feature to have wings coloured in vivid pink. The church fittings (pews, screen & pulpit) are Laudian and were completed in 1640, the same date as the font which is made of Portland stone. Being near Dorchester in Dorset, we have many tourists visiting the area who are delighted to see our lovely 'quintessentially English' village church.  *Janet Ranger-Dennis*

# St Mary's Church, Bridport

St Mary's has a strong bell ringing team of 15 ringers, but we only have 8 bells, recast and rehung between the wars, but we ring them as often as we can, sharing and swapping and learning.

The Covid pandemic stopped us in our tracks, but we gradually realised that the overlooked cupboard in the corner of the ringing chamber contained a magic system, the Ellacombe Apparatus. One of our longest serving ringers, Sam Dunn, had lovingly maintained it over the years, even though we did not appreciate its qualities till Covid struck.

Sam had rung it every year, especially to sound out happy Birthday to his ringer wife Brenda. In his honour, we renamed the Ellacombe Apparatus the Samathon, with apologies to its inventor, but felt the name needed personalising – sorry!

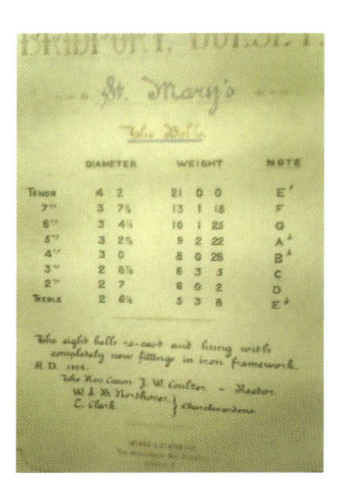

And in learning to ring the Samathon (Sorry, the Ellacombe Apparatus) we have tried to ring out some of the tunes that had been lovingly collected and written by earlier ringing teams, but found that ringing our traditional methods worked very well.

We do our best to publicise our ringing and the lovely church bells in St Mary's, and the local paper the Bridport News is a great help to tell our town what we are doing.

We plan to ring the bells fully, all together, on COVID UNLOCK day, Monday 21$^{st}$ June 2021, and also to ring the Samathon to do our part in the world wide rolling ring on Saturday June 26$^{th}$ 2021. We will greatly enjoy that, and hope the neighbours do too.      *Bob Hardwick*

*Ringer Tony Wakeling during Covid*

# St Mary the Virgin Swanage

The Church of St Mary the Virgin is the ancient parish church of Swanage. It is built of local Purbeck stone for which the district is famous and has seen Swanage grow from a small fishing hamlet to a popular Victorian seaside town. It was originally a chapel of ease for the neighbouring parish of Worth Matravers but became a parish with its own rector in 1487.

The church has been rebuilt on at least four occasions and the oldest remaining part is the tower.

The tower houses a fine ring of 8 bells, the tenor weighing just over 22cwt. The bells are hung for full-circle ringing and are rung regularly for services and practice sessions.

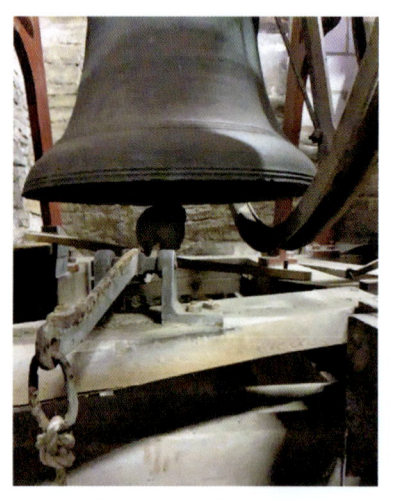

*Photo: Matthew Pike*

Until 1888, St Mary's church had only four bells, three by Wallis of Salisbury and the fourth by Lester and Pack of Whitechapel. In that year, the Wallis bells were re-tuned at Loughborough bellfoundry, the Whitechapel bell replaced and three trebles and a tenor added by John Taylor and Co., all dedicated to Mrs Elizabeth Burt. The new ring of eight bells was dedicated on 27th September 1888.

*Photo: Matthew Pike*

The Ellacombe apparatus was installed at some time after the augmentation and, despite infrequent use in recent years, has been kept in working order. However, the onset of the Covid-19 pandemic has restricted access to the ringing chamber and has seen a resurgence of Ellacombe chiming with a number of the regular ringers taking part on a rota basis, chiming for Sunday services, weddings and other special occasions.   *Rachael Rutter*

*Photo: Matthew Pike*

# Christchurch Priory, Christchurch

The Tower contains a ring of 12 bells, plus a flat 6th semi-tone bell, dating from the end of the 14th century to 1976. The two oldest, two of the oldest in England still in use, were cast in 1370 by a John Rufford of Bedfordshire, who was appointed the Royal Bellfounder by King Edward III in 1367. A medallion of the King's head is cast in the inscription on the crown band of each bell. This points to the fact that these bells, with others, were a royal gift to the Priory at Twynham. King's Head Bells as they are called, are very rare.

There is little doubt that the church at one time had a central tower. It is doubtful if the 7 bells referred to by Henry VIII in 1540 were ever in that central tower.. There are indications that the room over the Great North Porch was once a bell chamber The present tower was completed in 1470 and in due course the bells were hung there. The first reference to 8 bells is in a Vestry minute book of 1640

In 1885 "Ellacombe" chiming apparatus for ten bells was installed. This is still in use to-day and regularly used at Christmas, chiming Carols before the Crib Services at the Priory. And other appropriate occasions

A smaller "Ellacombe" apparatus was placed on the north side of the tower at ground floor level. This was used by the Countess of Malmesbury to sound a bell when she opened the restored peal of bells after they had been rededicated by the Vicar, Rev T.H. Bush, on 14 November 1885. This was mainly dismantled several years ago, but one rope remains attached to the Tenor Bell and is used regularly as a 'Sanctus Bell'

Some parts of the above taken from "The Story of Christchurch Bells" by Arthur V Davis

*Rosemary Rogers, Tower Captain*

EAST SUSSEX
# Holy Trinity, Coleman's Hatch

(8 bells, 11-2-2cwt in G. Cast by Gillett & Johnston 1913)

Holy Trinity Church stands on high ground and is clearly visible from all approaches. It has been fittingly described as "the cathedral of the country". Its size and capacity (seating 330) are out of proportion in relation to the hamlet that it serves. It is an architectural gem, built in local sandstone to a very high standard and with an unusually spacious interior.

The Church is located in the small hamlet of Coleman's Hatch, on a sharp bend on the north side of the B2110, almost equidistant between the villages of Forest Row and Hartfield, and some 2 miles from each. The parish of Coleman's Hatch (population around 700) is a quintessentially rural idyll comprising a scattering of farms, houses and cottages on the Northern fringes of the Ashdown Forest. 'Hatch' is a name for a gate or entrance to the forest.

The church was completed and consecrated in 1913 and the tower holds 8 bells, which were cast in 1913 by Gillett & Johnston.

They are regarded as one of the finest peals in Sussex, being surpassed possibly by nearby Withyham and Fairwarp. The bells are also fitted with an Ellacombe Chime system which was used on an ad-hoc basis for about 40 years leading up until 2020. Due to the COVID-19 pandemic, the bellringers could not meet to ring the bells so Ollie Watson, the youngest ringer in the band aged 16, got the chimes set up and has been ringing them for 30 minutes before the service on Sunday ever since.

During the pandemic, Ollie has started a project to restore the bells and Ellacombe chime and in August of 2021, the Ellacombe chime will be restored to commemorate the bicentenary of itsconception in Bitton, South Gloucestershire.
*Ollie Watson*

ESSEX

## St Peter's Goldhanger, Maldon

The Ellacombe Chimes frame in St. Peter's Goldhanger has a manufacturer's plate with a date of 1904. At that time there were six bells in the tower. When the bells were upgraded to 8 bells in 1951, unlike many other towers the Chimes facility was also upgraded to eight, using the original frame.

From hand written music scores in the tower which date back to the 1950s, we know that the chimes were used at that time to play carols at Christmas and appropriate hymns during Lent. Since then, there have been periods when the number of experienced full circle ringers has fallen to the level when playing the Ellacombe Chimes has been more appropriate for Sunday services. It is also often used to toll the tenor for mid-week funerals.

The front of the church has had no gravestones for over 100 years and it is maintained as an immaculate lawn in a prominent position in the middle of the village. Social and fund-raising events are frequently held on the lawn and the Ellacombe Chimes are played with a mix of secular well-known tune, rounds and call-changes. Eyebrows have been raised at the sound of Elvis Presley's "Can't Help Falling in Love" and Rod Stewart's "I am Sailing". With the Ellacombe frame just inside the tower door, children and their parents are invited to ring rounds.

A description and a photo of the Goldhanger device has for many years been included on the village history webpage plus examples of music scores. This resulted in requests for copies of the scores from several UK towers and in turn, with much encouragement and help from the Tower Captain of St. Mary's Church Clapham, resulted in the creation the Ellacombe Chimes Support website.     *David Newman*

## GLOUCESTERSHIRE
## Holy Trinity Church, Drybrook

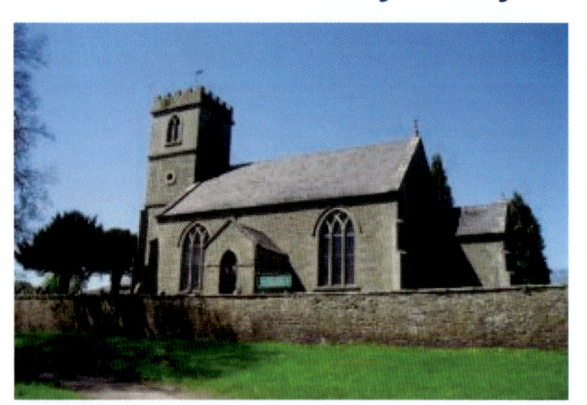

Holy Trinity church on Harrow Hill, Drybrook, (originally known as Harry Hill) was first used for worship on February 2nd. 1817. It was built to serve the surrounding communities, many of whom were involved in iron and coal mining.

In September 1919 a peal of 8 tubular bells was installed in the clock tower as a permanent memorial to the 47 men of the parish who gave their lives In the First World War of 1914-1918.

These are in addition to two full bells hung for chiming and were dedicated during a memorial service by the then Bishop of Gloucester, the Rt. Revd. Dr. Gibson. The tubular bells were cast by Harringtons of London at a cost of £130.

After 90 years of service to the parish, the bells were in need of refurbishment. They were also rotated so that the clapper would hit a different side and they would wear more evenly. This work was undertaken by Whites of Appleton Ltd. of Abingdon. To make the ringing more accessible the ringing frame was made and extended into the church porch by Maurice Bent and Robert Young, members of the congregation. A service of rededication, conducted by the Rt Revd. John Went, Bishop of Tewkesbury, was held on August 2nd. 2009, with many parts of the service following the order used in 1919.

The BBC programme 'Country file' visited the church for an episode broadcast in November 2012, highlighting the link between the bells and those in whose memory they had been installed, a programme aired in many countries around the world.

The bells continue to be rung regularly for Sunday services, weddings and funerals and are also much enjoyed by visiting children!

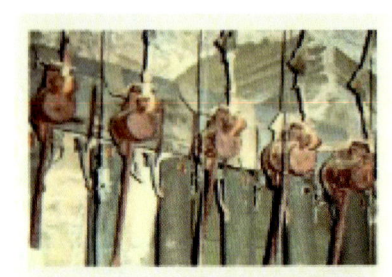

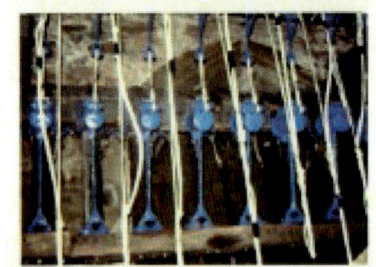

*Revd Clare Edwards*

## HAMPSHIRE
## St John's Church, Boldre

Boldre Church stands alone in a beautiful situation on the top of a hill near Lymington in the New Forest. It dates back to 987. Three bells were recorded in the inventory of 1552. In 1928 five more bells were added.

It is thought that the Ellacombe chiming apparatus was installed at this time.

The bells are fixed static in the tower and so it is not possible to use them for conventional change-ringing. The Ellacombe chimes are rung regularly before services and after weddings.

*Carol Edge*

105

# St. Peter & Holy Cross Church, Wherwell

The tower holds a peal of five bells originally cast by William and Rob Cor in 1707 with a tenor weighing 7cwt. These were transferred from a Norman church previously on the site which due to its dilapidated state was replaced in 1858 with a church designed by Henry Woodyer. This church was described by Pevsner as being lively, with a rather Scandinavian bell-turret with spire! For reasons that are not clear the bells when re-rung were placed in a two tier frame which ultimately became the problem and resulted in the peal deemed to be unsafe for full circle ringing, with the last full peal rung on 18th April 1993.

In 2012 major works were undertaken to replace the nave roof and renew the spire. At the same time the Victorian bell frame was repaired and strengthened ahead of a further drive to bring the bells back to full circle ringing. However money became a major issue and this was put on hold. However, with the advice and help of Alan Hughes of Whitechapel Bell Foundry, the Ellacombe Chimes were manufactured and installed so that the village would again be able to hear, as described by the incumbent, the *'voice of the church'*.

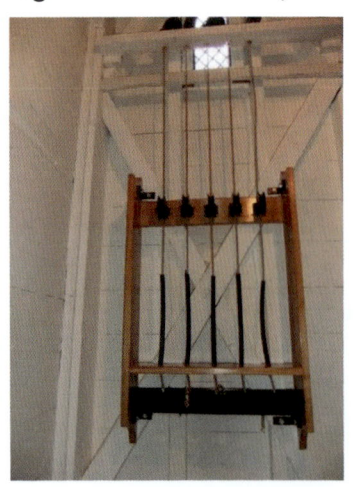

We now have a team of nine chimers who, before the pandemic, met regularly to practice every second Tuesday and then chime for the Sunday services and on special occasions. To date we have rung at over 40 weddings.

We enjoy the flexibility that the Ellacombe offers with Call changes, Double method ringing and a varied selection of hymns particularly over Christmas and Lent composed for chiming by our church organist, who also composed the 'specials' such as 'Keep the Home Fires Burning' and 'It's a Long Way to Tipperary' for the Armistice Day commemoration in 2018. We also participated in the Martin Creed Olympic Composition of 'Five Ring Doubles'.

*David Etchells*

# The Abbey Church of St Mary and St Ethelflaeda, Romsey

The Abbey Church of St Mary and St Ethelflaeda can trace its origins back to 907 AD, the year in which King Edward the Elder, son of the Saxon King Alfred the Great, first settled a small number of nuns there under the charge of his daughter Elflaeda.

The first stone church and nunnery were built c. 1000 AD and work began on the present building c. 1120-1140.

There are eight bells in the wooden octagonal belfry or lantern which sits on top of the tower. There have been bells at the Abbey since 1624 and the present ring were cast in 1791 by Thomas Mears, a Bell Founder in London. The heaviest bell, the Tenor, weighs 22 CWT and has the note of Db.

An Ellacombe apparatus is present on the West side of the ringing chamber. It is not known exactly when this was installed however it bears the name Mears and Stainbank who were master Founders at the Whitechapel Bell Foundry from 1865 to 1873 so it is reasonable to assume that installation was during this period. There are no records to indicate how frequently it was used initially.

Over the last few decades, it has been used very occasionally for services during the working day and on one occasion to play carols on Christmas day. However, in 2020 when social distancing measures to combat the Coronavirus pandemic prevented normal bellringing, the Ellacombe has been used regularly to chime the bells for Sunday service and weddings.

The Abbey, its bellringers and the people of Romsey are grateful to have this special bit of Victorian history which has sat quietly in the background for years and now has really proved its worth and brought joy in difficult times. There is no doubt that it will be used much more frequently in the future.

*Alistair Brown*

# HERTFORDSHIRE
## St Peter's, Ayot St Peter

St Peter's is a listed Victorian Church in the "arts and crafts" style that has been carefully maintained over the years and is in exceptional and original condition.

*Photo courtesy V. Richards*

The church features in the Simon Jenkins book "England's Thousand Best Churches" (1999). It was designed by the noted architect John Pollard Seddon and completed in 1875. It has a fine font, pulpit and a beautiful painted ceiling in the chancel. It also features the only church commission undertaken by the famous Martin Brothers pottery.

The bells are a diatonic chime of six which were cast at the former London foundry of John Warner and Sons in 1875 and are all connected to the Ellacombe unit. An inscription on the waist of the 3rd bell records the fact that the bells were given by Henry Jephson MD in memory of Eliza Jephson. The Ellacombe frame is located in a small room on the first floor of the church tower.

The current church is at least the fourth in the parish - the previous structures were built on a different site to the north, where an old churchyard still exists. The last church on the old site was struck by lightning on Friday 10 July 1874 and largely destroyed by fire. There was a great sense of urgency about the provision of a replacement.

The foundation stone – which came from the doorway of the destroyed church – was laid on 7 April 1875 not by Lord Cowper (as it says) but by his wife; he was unwell on the appointed day.

The disused railway line known as the Ayot Greenway is an attractive destination for walkers and National Cycle Route 12 runs through the parish, making it popular with cyclists too.

The area around the church has an approximate postcode of AL6 9BG. *David Morgan*

*Photo courtesy S. Trendell*

# St George's, Anstey

St George's is a Grade 1 medieval building dating from the 12$^{th}$ Century, (c.1170). The Church appears in the book "Britain's 1000 Best Churches" and receives many visitors from the U.K. and abroad, particularly the U.S. as there is a wartime connection with a U.S. airfield nearby. A millenium memorial window, depicting a mass of butterflies flying into a sky filled with bomber aircrafts is dedicated to the American airman who gave their lives in World War 11.

Records show a flint and rubble church stood here in Saxon times. It was rebuilt around 1200 by Sir Richard de Anestie whose ornate but damaged tomb is in the church. Some of the material from the castle which stood behind the church is thought to have been incorporated in the building.

*Five of the Anstey Ringers/Chimers*

The church is noted for its abundance of early graffiti, including some from the 13th century and shows military helmets and shields and that of an Elizabethan man. The Norman font is one of only two known in England to be decorated with mermen holding their tails.

The church is of cruxiform design and the Central Tower holds a ring of six bells, the earliest being from the 15th Century and the last from 1778. All ringing is done from the crossing as the vicar at the time was concerned about shenanigans up the tower.

The chimes have been particularly useful during the Covid pandemic as it has enabled Anstey to continue ringing for services, weddings and funerals.

*Alison Norfolk*

# HUNTINGDONSHIRE
## St. John the Baptist, Holywell-cum-Needingworth

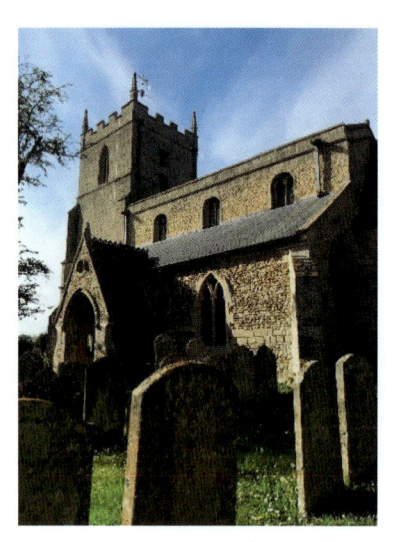

There has been a ring of bells at St. John the Baptist Holywell-cum-Needingworth since at least 1625. However, by the start of the 20th century both the wooden bell frame and the bells themselves were in very poor condition. The bells had not been used for full-circle ringing since the late 1700s and earlier attempts to create a more stable frame were damaging the structure of the tower. Following a decision to reinstate full circle ringing a new metal frame was installed by Taylors of Loughborough in 1915, three of the original bells were reused, a fourth was recast to create a new tenor and a new treble was added. At the same time an Ellacombe Chimes frame and associated hammers were installed. The bell frame and the Ellacombe frame allowed augmentation to 6 bells, which took place in 1946 with the addition of a new treble (making the new treble from 1915 the new No 2 bell).

Since augmentation to 6 bells Holywell has been primarily a full-circle ringing tower with over 100 peals and numerous Quarters rung in the past 75 years. The Ellacombe chimes have been more occasionally used, particularly when a band was not available for Sunday service. During the past year it has proven very fortuitous that the chimes had been kept in good working order as full circle ringing has effectively ceased. Hymns, popular tunes and other pieces are now chimed regularly by myself and have resulted in numerous positive comments from parishioners. With only 6 bells available it can be a challenge devising suitable arrangements of hymns, a challenge that my wife has fortunately taken on, and we continue to seek new possibilities.

Within the churchyard is an enclosed well (hence 'Holywell') and for many years the well has been dressed using flower petals on clay boards as part of the annual patronal festival in late June. This is not a local tradition but was started by a former incumbent who hailed from Derbyshire, where well dressing potentially traces its origins back to the Black Death epidemic in the 14th century. How remarkable therefore that all these centuries later Ellacombe Chimes should be bringing pleasure to those living through a pandemic.

*Roger Beaman Tower Captain*

# ISLE OF MAN
## St Thomas', Douglas

The original peal of 6 bells was presented to St. Thomas by Rev. R. Cattley, Curate of Kirk Onchan, who assisted the Chaplain of St Thomas' in 1852.

On December 3rd, 1852, a team of nine ringers from Liverpool rang a peal of 5,040 changes in 2 hours 47 minutes.

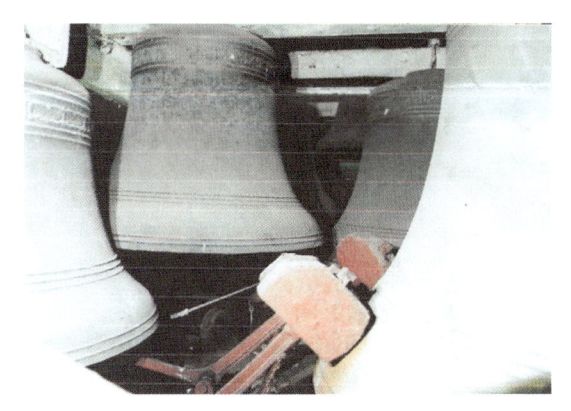

A fire in the tower on 11th February 1912 destroyed the bells. However, they were recast and replaced later that year. An additional 2 bells were added in 1926 to complete the octave.

The peal is hung stationary (not swung) in a steel framework and the bells are played by one person sing an Ellacombe apparatus.

In the church Year Book of 1928 - 29 there is an article which states that, *'the eight bells are cast of best quality bell-metal, copper and tin alloy and are accurately tuned to equal temperament on Messrs. Taylor's special "true harmonic" system, which, stated briefly, means that the overtones, or harmonics, of the bells are controlled so as to bear a definite musical relationship to the fundamental tone; this ensures great sweetness and purity of tonal effect'.*

KENT
# St. Michael and All Angels, Tenterden

St. Michael's is a Victorian church on the North side of Tenterden, an old Wealden market town. The church has the unusual distinction of having given its name to the village which has grown up around it and which was previously known as Boresisle The church was built in 1863 and initially the tower stopped at the level just below the spire which was added in 1866. The bells were given in 1892 by Mrs. Gordon, widow of Admiral Gordon, and she was a great benefactor to the church.

The ring of six is hung with the bells fixed to the frame so they were only ever intended to be rung by means of the Ellacombe machine which is at the base of the tower in the choir vestry. They were cast by Gillett & Co, and they are in G with a tenor of 10 cwt. The biggest problem with them is that the local jackdaws build their nests on the stone louvres and, despite the wire netting inside the louvres, the floor of the bellchamber is always piled high with sticks.

Nowadays the bells are rung only on special occasions, though until recently they were rung regularly for Sunday service. The principal ringer is Melanie Critchell who has been ringing the bells for over fifty years, and in the past she has been aided by Moira Duncombe (nee Crosser), Raymond Crawfurd, Richard Edwards tower captain of the town church of St. Mildred's, and other ringers from St. Mildred's.

On the day of the bicentenary, June 26th 2021, there will be a wedding in church at 2pm, and to ring the bells at 12 midday as well would be bound to cause confusion so they will be rung for the 2pm service instead.

*Raymond Crawfurd*

# Saints Peter and Paul, Borden

Restoration of the Borden Church Ellacombe apparatus wasn't easy. We were fortunate in finding a bellringer, Graham, who chimed an Ellacombe in his own tower and liked the idea of working on ours as an interesting project. We still had the original hammers and some of the frame, but we couldn't find replacement pulleys, so he made them himself.

Borden Churchwarden, Kathy, ran North Kent Joinery, at the Brunel Sawmill in the Historic Chatham Dockyard, and they made and donated some pieces of joinery that we needed for the Ellacombe. Marc Brunel, father of Isambard Kingdom Brunel, was the architect of the Sawmill. It was only after our Ellacombe restoration was completed that we learnt that Henry Ellacombe, pursuing a career in engineering and working under Brunel at the Dockyard, oversaw the work of the building of the sawmill. It was a delightful surprise to discover that vital parts of our Ellacombe apparatus were made at a sawmill where Henry Ellacombe himself supervised the building.

Borden has a keen band of bellringers that the Rev. Ellacombe would surely have disapproved of, frequenting as we do the Maypole Inn, which itself has historic connections with the casting of our bells. Having a regular band of ringers, it wasn't realised that the Borden Ellacombe would ever have an important or necessary role and it was used mainly to chime Carols at Christmas. However, during the year of the pandemic and consequent restrictions on group activities, bellringing stopped and the bells of many churches have been silent. It is thanks to our Ellacombe that our beloved Borden bells continued to ring. When normal service resumes for bellringing, our Ellacombe will continue to be used and treasured and known for its service to the Church and Parish, keeping the bells ringing throughout the crisis.

*Vivien Smith*

# St Michael and All Angels, Hartlip
Ring of six

The Ellacombe chiming apparatus in Hartlip was installed in December 1908. The Hartlip tower is cramped. As a result, the hammers for the Ellacombe are not quite at right-angles to the axis of rotation of the bell. So, with a long piece of chiming, the bells begin to rock backwards and forwards, which makes for more difficult timing.

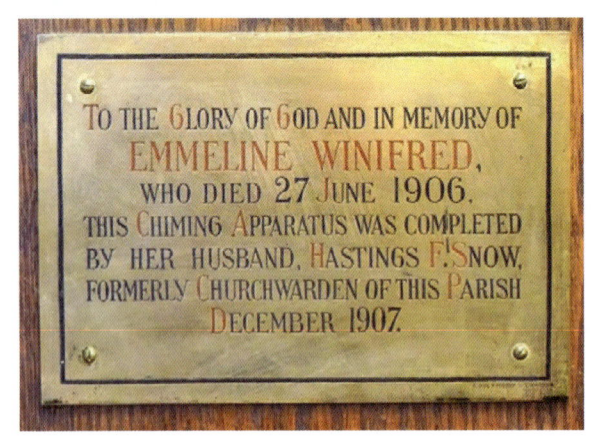

The vicar of Hartlip before and after the First World War annotated the Register of Services in great detail.

He seems to have had a somewhat fractious relationship with the bellringers. On November the 14th 1909 he noted "Ringers refused to attend the services and therefore resigned. Chiming bracket now used." For a number of weeks the words "Chiming Bracket" are entered in the Register.

In September 1911 he wrote, "After a meeting in the Vicarage on September 20th vicar said, 'Belfry at your disposal on condition ringers attend Church on Sunday as far as is possible." The entry for the 24th suggests that the ringers were pleased as the Register shows that the bells were rung for one hour for both the morning and evening services.

In more recent times the "bracket" has seen use for service ringing. The local primary school holds its Friday assemblies in the Church. For a number of years, three pupils from the top class would be chosen to ring the chiming machine before the service. With the six notes Kumbaya needs no alteration but the most popular tune was a version of "Happy Birthday", played if any of the children had a birthday that week.

The only worry was that the more enthusiastic members of the young band would try ringing the bells as loudly as possible by pulling the chiming ropes as hard as they could. *Peter Blandon*

# Sacred Heart Church, Sittingbourne

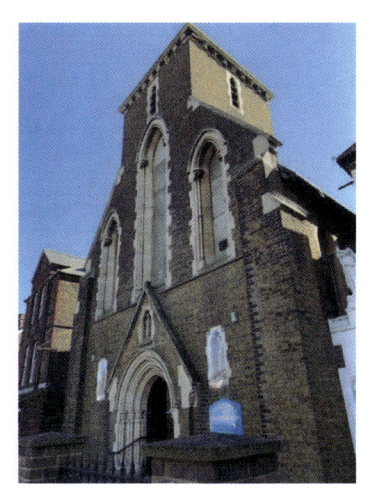

In 1905 a chime of eight bells, with a flat 2nd and 4th, was installed and hung in the tower in a frame on two levels. They were cast by Felix Aerschodt of Louvain, Belgium. According to the nuns still resident in the parish, the bells were acquired so that a composition by the Mother Superior could be rung.

The bells are originally listed as having been rung by a mechanical device. It was only after the first world war, after years of disuse, that they were converted to 'Ellacombe style' manual ringing (in 1925). At one point, the bells were rung by electronic solenoid hammers although these have not been used for many years. In 1983, the six diatonic bells were taken out of the tower and stored at the Whitechapel Bell foundry pending restoration.

However, due to a lack of funds they remained there until the year 2000, when the restoration finally took place. The bells were tuned and a new treble and tenor cast to create a diatonic set of 8 bells ringable by an 'Ellacombe style' apparatus (see picture – taken after they had been reinstalled).

The work that took place in 2000 led to a fine ring of bells. The melodious sound of the bells drift all over the centre of the town on a Sunday morning and some weekday mornings before the Mass. Plain hunt, rounds and call changes and many hymns and Christmas carols are rung on the bells. 'Little donkey' is a favourite all the year round! The tower has built up an impressive collection of 'scores' covering a variety of hymns, meaning we have tunes suitable for every liturgical season. It is hoped the bells will continue to ring for many years to come. *Stephen Trafford*

## St Peter's Ightham

The small, beautiful church of St Peter's is Grade 1 listed and was first mentioned in 1122 in the Textus Roffensis. It has close links with nearby Ightham Mote and in its chancel there is a very fine effigy of the house's first owner, Sir Thomas Cawne, who died in about 1374. There are also splendid monuments to Dame Dorothy Selby (1641), her husband Sir William (1611) and his nephew Sir William (1638), who also owned the Mote. Other significant items in the church include the great door (c1550), the double tier chandelier (1759), the box pews (early 1600s) and the 12 funeral hatchments.

The church has six bells ranging in weight from the treble at 198kg to the tenor at 445kg. The 3 and 4, cast by John Walgrave, are believed to date from around 1430 and at least one is thought to be original. The tenor, which was re-cast in 1937, was originally made or re-cast in 1620 by John Wilnar.

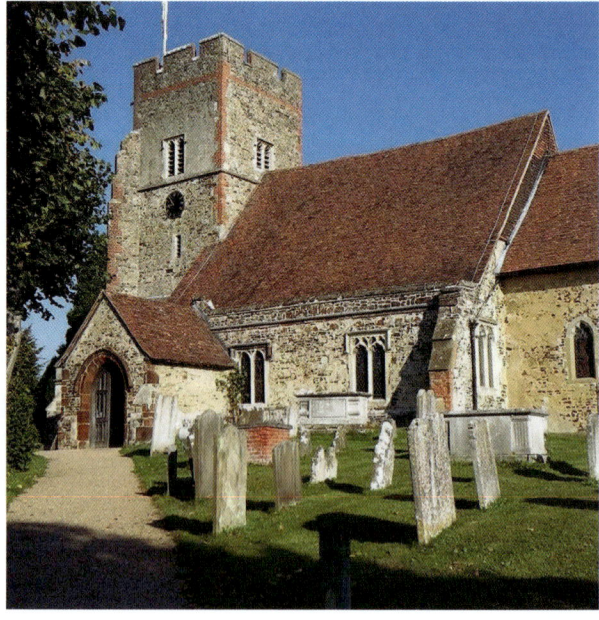

The church's Victorian Ellacombe chimes are played whilst seated and the distance from the pulleys to the bottom of the ropes is more than 1m, so the ropes are pulled from 2/3 of the way down rather than in the middle. Ightham ringers have only recently discovered, thanks to the Ellacombe Chimes Support Group, that this is unusual. The configuration may have been to prevent ringers from striking too hard, or to enable children to ring safely. The Support Group has suggested moving the tubes up the ropes so that the chimes may be played more conventionally. This will be implemented after the chimes are rung for the 200th anniversary celebration.

*Judith Robinson*

## LANCASHIRE
# Saint George's Church, Chorley

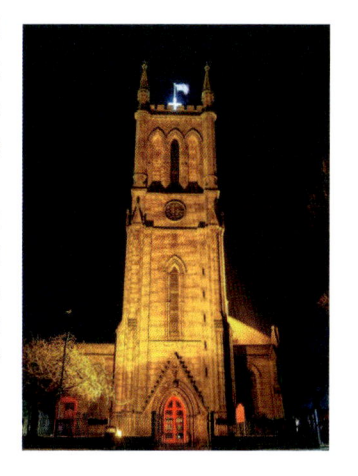

The Tower at Saint George's Church in Chorley has ten fixed hemispherical Ellacombe Chimes by Mears and Stainbank (1919). The Chimes are a registered War Memorial and were installed to honour those from the Parish who died during the First World War.

> "It is with deep gratitude to the men who gave up Father and Mother, Sisters and Brothers, Wife and Children, Relatives and Friends, Home and Country for us that we might live, that a permanent memorial may be erected to remind us of the great Sacrifice that has been made. May we ever live lives worthy of such a Sacrifice".

**April 1919, The Messenger, Parish Magazine**

The Chimes were restored in 2013 from a donation made by Mr John Collinson in memory of his beloved Wife, Denise. The work was undertaken by Taylors of Loughborough.

The Ellacombe Chimes are played regularly for Sunday Services and Weddings. The Chimes are a popular attraction during Heritage Weekends where the Public can also ring the Chimes! The Tower Captain Dr Victoria Gibson has 35 years of Ellacombe Chime & Change Ringing experience and teaches 18 children to play hymns and adapted peals on the Chimes for Church Services. The Ellacombe Chimes at Saint George's Church have featured in two BBC programmes. The first in 2015, for The One Show with presenter, Angellica Bell, and in 2020 on the local BBC News featuring Ellacombe Chimes being played during the Covid Pandemic. *Dr Victoria Gibson*

**Angellica Bell** @angellicabell

Now at #StGeorgesChurch in #Chorley ringing #EllacombeChimes with @DrVGibson - the bells sounded great! #TheOneShow

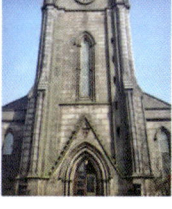

# LEICESTERSHIRE
## St Catherine of Alexandria, Burbage

For a little over 800 years the Parish Church of Burbage, dedicated to St Catherine of Alexandria, has stood on its present spot, its tall spire dominating the hill. The known history of the bells commences in 1701 when three were present in the tower. In 1761 these were augmented to five. In 1924 the bells were inspected by Taylor's of Loughborough and a Mr Oldham pronounced them to be "absolutely unsafe". Efforts got underway to recast the ring, augment it to eight and refurbish the tower.

On 21st January 1925 a village meeting was held in the Co-op Hall and an appeal was launched to raise the funds for the work. A number of the villagers requested that one of the bells was to be in memory of those Burbage men who died in the Great War.

Contributions flooded in and £1,083 5s was raised, more than the amount required for the work to be carried out, in fact when everything was completed, including costs of the dedication service £10 2s was left over. The completion of the work took approximately 5 months.

The Ellacombe frame must have been installed at the same time, but there are no records of this. The frame was installed on the new ringing floor.

In the 1950's the ringers became aware of the Verger, who using the Ellacombe Chimes, was ringing for weddings and keeping the fee. So, the Tower Captain removed the frame and moved it into the Clock room, rendering it unusable.

Major repair works were carried out on the tower in 2008 meaning the bells could not be rung, so the Ellacombe frame was installed clock room and was used to call people to worship. Throughout the lockdown periods, with the permission of the incumbent, the Ellacombe Chimes have been used, much to the appreciation of the local community. *Martin Mellor*

## LONDON
## St Andrew's, Hornchurch

At St Andrew's, Hornchurch, 8 of our 10 bells are fitted with Ellacombe chimes operated from a traditional chiming frame in the ringing room.

When the bells were augmented from 6 to 8 in 1901, a wooden frame remained and it wasn't until a metal frame was installed by Taylor's in 1909 that we think the 8 Ellacombe chimes were introduced. Our augmentation from 8 to 10 in 2001 did not include the installation of additional chimes for the 2 new trebles.

Our living memory of using the Ellacombe chimes goes back to 1958. At this time, the wooden beams supporting our copper spire had become infested with deathwatch beetle and were going rotten. During the period 1958 – 1962 the tower was deemed too unsafe for full bell ringing but chiming was permitted whilst a concrete ring was installed to support the spire.

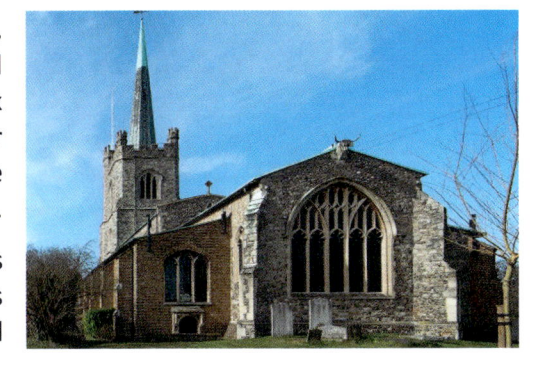

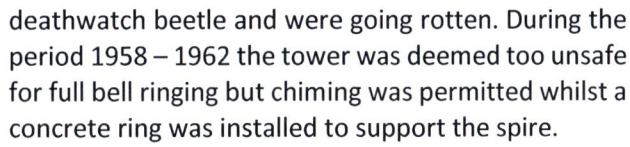

Our ringing master of the time, Frank Gant, took on the role of chiming for services and weddings whilst still maintaining a band by ringing at other towers. One of our current members, Tony Ammerlaan, reports that Frank Gant chimed the bells for his wedding to Joyce in 1961. Tony was taught to ring by Frank in 1953 and still rings (and chimes) today.

For the 200th Anniversary of the chimes, Tony performed the 'Z – Cars' theme tune as a tribute to Frank who, himself, enjoyed playing that tune.

The congregation of the time commented that they preferred the tune ringing to the traditional bell ringing but, with a strong band maintained ever since, there has been little use made of the chimes until the Coronavirus Pandemic of 2020/21. With various restrictions on bell ringing during the pandemic, our Ellacombe chimes have again been used for services and weddings. *Clive Stephenson*

*Tony Ammerlaan, Hornchurch chimes*

## Our Immaculate Lady of Victories ('St.Mary's'), Clapham

Mr. Soltau, a staunch Anglican, lived in the left-hand portion of the mansion formerly owned by Lord Teignmouth in which the "abolitionist" Clapham Sect and other important social reformers had been based.

**Rev.de Held's Tower:** The locals wanted nothing to do with Catholics generally, but especially the hundreds of impoverished Irish refugees who were ending up in Clapham. Rev.de Held and his Redemptorist colleagues came to minister to the refugees and the other Catholics in the area.

They acquired the right-hand portion of the mansion, mounted a bell cote on their end, and started bonging away while building their new "chapel" (it couldn't be called a church before Catholic Emancipation). Mr. Soltau was seriously aggrieved by all this.

**Soltau's home and de Held's new tower:** Six relatively large bells had been built into the tower during construction. They began ringing at 5:00am on the day of the Consecration of the new building in 1851. (The

*Mr.Soltau's home behind new belfry*

early start was in order to 'avoid violent protests by the non-Catholic majority in the area'!)

Mr. Soltau really "lost it" when they were heard many times every day, always beginning at 5:00am. The resulting court case, "Soltau v. de Held", is an important precedent in English Law which is still cited around the World in cases relating to Church bells and other noise nuisances. He obtained an injunction, so the bells would be silent until he either moved out or died.

He refused to sell his half to the Redemptorists for years but they were later able to build the transept on the site.

I suspect the bells were originally chimed randomly in the continental manner, so Towers now defending cases against modern full-circle bell-ringing might be able to get the precedent "distinguished".

*Mike Shelley*

## St. James's Church, Hampton Hill

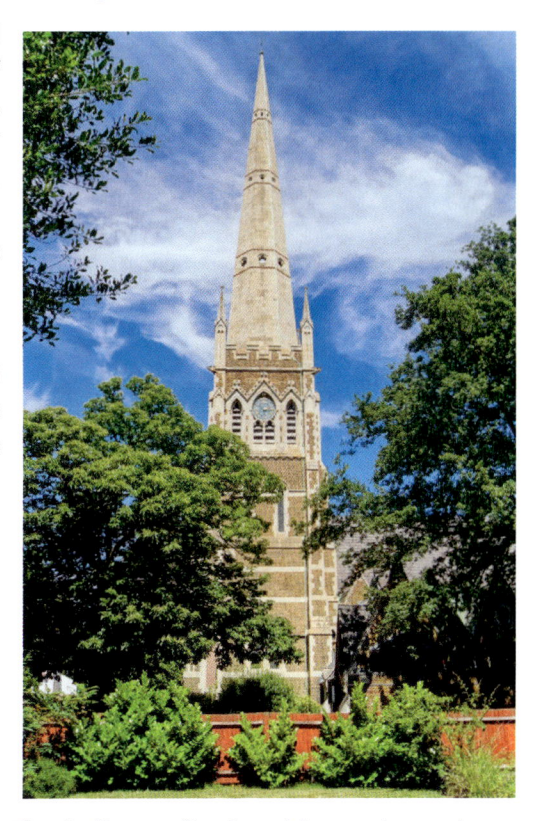

The original church, consisting of a nave, chancel and small vestry, was built in 1863. As the population of the parish grew, it was extended over the next 25 years. Queen Victoria's golden jubilee in 1887 prompted the construction of the tower and spire. The clock and four bells were installed in 1893 and a further two bells were added in 1902 to mark the coronation of King Edward VII. Each bell is inscribed with a verse from the Bible.

The ringing frame has room for 8 ropes but only 6 bells were ever installed. The firm which made the original bells no longer exists so new matching bells cannot be acquired.

The bells are fixed and have always been rung by the Ellacombe chimes method. Bells 3 to 6 are used for the automatic chiming of the clock, by external clappers at the back. The internal clappers on all the bells are for manual ringing. The ringing and clock areas are above the baptistry and accessed by a spiral staircase, but a rope passing through the floor enables bell 6 to be tolled from ground-floor level.

The bells are rung every Sunday and for weddings, midnight mass at Christmas and to ring in the New Year. Additionally, they are rung on special occasions which may be personal (eg. wedding anniversaries) or national (eg. jubilees). Every year in July we hold a St. James's Festival weekend when visitors can try ringing the bells and climb the spire to admire the view; Wembley Stadium and the Shard are visible on a clear day. *Susan Horner*

## St Nicholas Church - Chislehurst

St Nicholas Church was built in the 15th century and enlarged in the 19th, though a church has been on the site for over a thousand years. The 15th century rebuilding incorporated the west wall of the earlier church, and a small Saxon window is visible outside above the West door. The Norman font is still in use.

The Rood Screen survives from the 15th century; but its loft was removed at the Reformation. The screen encloses the Scadbury Chapel and the Walsingham Tomb. Thomas Walsingham is attributed with the rebuilding of the church in the 'Perpendicular' style. Sir Francis Walsingham was spymaster to Queen Elizabeth.

The Tower and Spire were rebuilt after the originals were destroyed by fire in 1857. The broached spire, clad in cedar shingles, (formerly oak), is 111ft high to the weathercock. The bells cast by Warners date from then and incorporate metal from the earlier bells destroyed in the fire. They are rung from the tower floor. Above that is the clock room which houses the Ellacombe apparatus and the clock by Dent.

Edmund Denison, later Lord Grimthorpe was involved initially in the restoration of the bells; but withdrew when insistence was given to the replacement of the original six bells by eight. However, he did install Dent's clock that they had designed for the Palace of Westminster, ('Big Ben'). This remains, in its original condition, with the addition of electrical winding, the first to use his Grimthorpe Escapement and keeping 'time' to within one second a week.

The Churchyard contains graves of some notable people including: Sir Malcolm Campbell; William Willett, originator of Summer Time, and Fr Charles Lowder, first Vicar of St Peter's, London Docks.

*Peter Appleby*

MERSEYSIDE
# St Peter's, Formby

The Ancient Chapelry of Formby was in existence prior to 1650. In the middle of the 18th Century the folk of Formby decided to build a new chapel as the original had fallen into a bad state of repair and it was also quite a distance from the dwelling houses of the inhabitants in the Chapelry.

The new Chapel was completed on the present site of St Peter's in 1746 and consecrated in 1747.

At the beginning of the 19th Century the church was extended and the building has remained externally much the same to the present day.

The Church tower houses a tolling bell, which was cast in 1695, and a set of 8 chimes. Up to the mid 1990's, the chimes were regularly used at services and often operated by some of the choirboys. However, because of the very narrow and steep staircase leading to the ringing chamber and the Ellacombe Frame, it was felt that there was a safety issue; usage of the chimes ceased, and they remained silent for a number of years.

In 2009, after an inspection of the Bell Tower and the framework of the tolling bell and the chimes, it was decided to refurbish the system and install solenoid operated hammers to sound the chimes. The hammers would be activated through a control box mounted conveniently on a wall inside the Church building. Changes and tunes can now be stored and played back at the touch of a button.

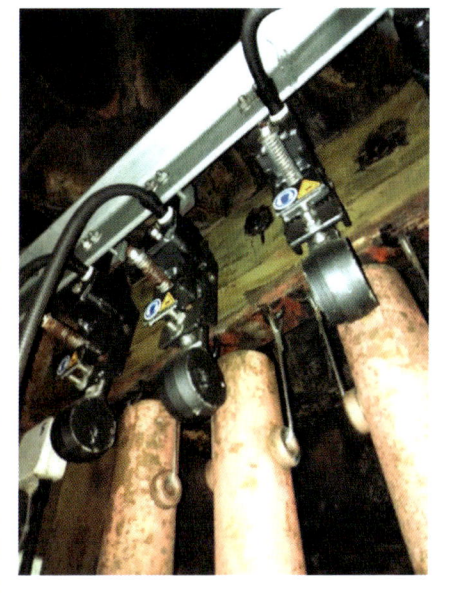

We currently have 6 Changes and around 30 tunes on the system. Appropriate Changes and tunes are grouped for continuous playback on special days such as Easter, Christmas, Weddings, etc.

*Mike Hastie*

## St Bridget's West Kirby

The church of St Bridget's in West Kirby is one of the oldest Wirral churches. Apart from having an excellent band of ringers our tower has the only bell cast by Bathgate and Wilson.

In the early 1700's the tower was rebuilt and in 1719 Abraham Rudal installed a ring of five bells. Many years later, in 1889 the bells were augmented to eight and we presume this was when Taylor's also supplied our chiming apparatus. We are now the only tower on the peninsula to have a working Ellacombe chime.

Around forty years ago one of our ringers had the foresight to have our Ellacombe chiming apparatus overhauled. Fortunately our underused resource became a well-used item during the lockdown period.

We have now been using our Ellacombe chime on all those Sunday mornings that we couldn't have our normal full circle ringing. Some of our more musical ringers have played tunes that have been recognised by the congregation. All the rest of us just ring changes and the congregation may now recognise *Queens & Whittingtons* chiming out.

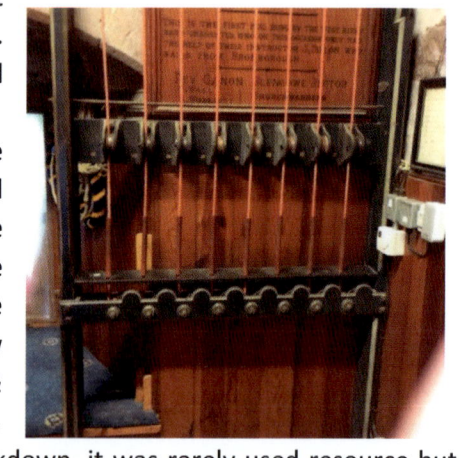

Before this pandemic lockdown, it was rarely used resource but with a shortage of ringers who were allowed to ring it has often been used to announce that the church is open. We plan to use it more often in the future.

We may have the only chime with its own guard dog. We often have visiting ringers, if you arrange a ringing or chiming outing and would like to visit us, call or text Janet (who took the photo of the church) 07863797743.

*Randle Tinkler, Tower Captain.*

NORFOLK
# Our Lady Saint Mary, South Creake

There have been bells at Saint Mary's since the early fourteenth century when the present tower was built. Originally there were three large bells but by 1552 records show that the ring had been augmented with two more bells. Finally in 1826 the five old bells were melted down and recast as the current bells by the respected Norfolk bell founder, William Dobson of Downham. For over four hundred years these five bells called villagers to worship but even before WWII they had fallen into disrepair and, whilst individual bells were occasionally chimed, they were silent thereafter as a full ring.

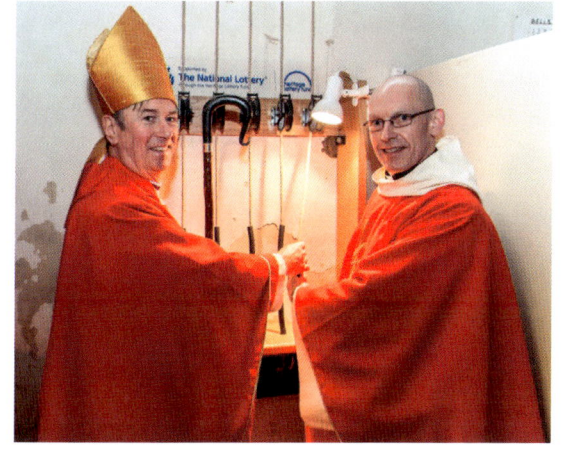

In 2014 with generous funding from the National Heritage Lottery Fund, an Ellacombe Chiming Apparatus was installed by the Whitechapel Bell Foundry and the bells were rededicated and blessed by the Bishop of Lynn in December of that year. The bells are now regularly chimed by a rota of ringers before Sunday worship and at weddings and funerals.

The historically important mediaeval frame, probably constructed in the early 14th century, has been adapted and changed over the centuries and, whilst no longer strong enough for the bells to be rung full circle, now continues to be used.

When the Ellacombe Apparatus was installed, the opportunity was also taken to reinstate the ringing of the Angelus at midday and 6.00pm by fitting an electronic striker to the treble bell. This mediaeval tradition was revived in South Creake in the 1920's but had lapsed some years ago. The bell is rung in three sets of three with a final nine rings.

# St. Mary's Church Baconsthorpe

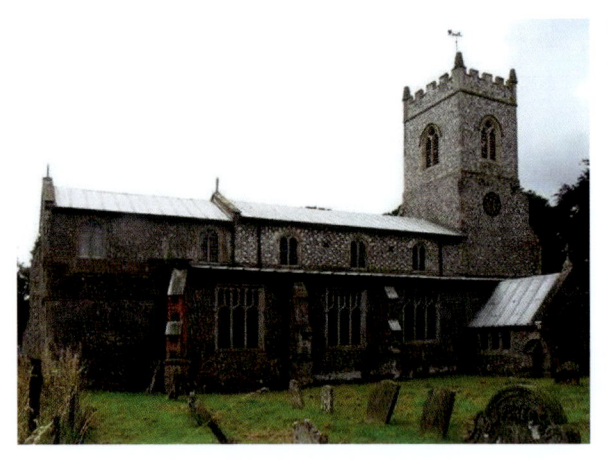

Baconsthorpe lies three miles south east of the Georgian market town of Holt. It is a small village with one hundred and five households and a population of just over two hundred.

St. Mary's Church is a focal part of the village that has provided pastoral care to generations of families still living in the village today.

According to the Doomsday Book of 1086 there was a church in Baconsthorpe attached to one of the Lordships which belonged to Robert Grenon that was endowed with 30 acres of land, 80 sheep and 40 goats. The earliest parts of the present church date from the 13th century and stand on Saxon foundations. Two of the arcades in the nave nearest the chancel are of the decorated style used between 1290-1350.

The church is a large building of flint and freestone. White flints have been knapped and squared and laid in courses, these are intended to reflect the early morning and late evening sunshine which will catch the eye from a distance.

The square western embattled tower collapsed in 1739, damaging the nave, roof and font. Repairs to the nave were started immediately, using the money from selling the two broken bells. The tower was not fully repaired until 1788.

There is one bell which bears the inscription "Charles Newman made me 1701", from which a large piece had broken off from the bottom accounting for the dull sound of the bell only heard when the clock chimed. In 1992 the bell was repaired by a local farmer, Roger Hall, in memory of his parents. There are also eight tubular bells erected in 1892 at a cost of £200.00.

# All Saint's Old Buckenham

All Saint's Old Buckenham is a thatched church (both nave and chancel) which has faced out onto a very large village green since the 11th century. The octagonal exterior of the tower, either replacing or facing a saxon round tower dates from the early 1300s so the tower has been an important lookout post over the surrounding countryside for at least 700 years.

The six bells are dated 1757 (recast in 1961), 1757, 1722, 1622, 1772 and 1772. Ranging in weight from just over three to just over eight hundredweight, they were originally hung for full circle ringing, and were rung like this until at least 1880.

Repairs were needed after the spire blew down in 1895, and not long after a report was made (by William Weir, an architect working for Prince Duleep Singh of Old Buckenham Hall) about a crack on the west face from under the belfry windows – caused he thought by the vibration of the bell frame.

In 1961 the old framework was removed and a properly designed chiming frame with steel joists made by Taylors of Loughborough was installed.

127

## NORTH YORKSHIRE
## All Saints' Bolton Percy

Nestled in a peaceful, tranquil churchyard in the quiet North Yorkshire village of Bolton Percy, All Saints' is a large church with a long history.

Consecrated in 1424 All Saints' was built on the site of an earlier church by the initiative of Canon Thomas Parker who was Rector from 1411 to 1423. Parker used the same architectural ideas and the same first-class material as can be found in York Minster. He also employed Minster workmen for the construction of All Saints'. It was doubtless the size, the lofty and spacious interior of All Saints coupled with the particularly fine quality of the chancel that has earned it the name of 'Cathedral of the Ainsty'.

The Church Bells, of which there are three, date back to the 17th Century with the Tenor Bell "The Great Bell of Bolton" being the oldest. Cracked in 1596 it was re-cast in 1605. The treble is dated 1760 and the middle bell is dated 1629. Nestled in an ancient oak frame the three bells were used throughout the years up to 1978 when they were rung "full-circle" for the last time. Deemed then too dangerous to be rung in that manner due to rot and decay the mechanisms were adapted so that ringing could continue by the method of "clocking".

Thanks to the Heritage Lottery Fund and other grant providers the required funds were raised and in May 2018 the bells were removed, restored and all the mechanisms and fittings replaced. An electronic Tempora system was also provided.

The All Saints' Bellringing team currently comprises 12 keen ringers with ages ranging from 18 to 80 and with a minimum of 15 weddings every year plus all the routine services they are all fully employed.

*Alan Swain*

*The bells after their restoration and about to be re-installed (May 2018); shows a few of the ringers who helped with the removal and re-installation; Bell Captain Martin Rice far left, Alan Swain far right.*

# St Mary's Goathland, Whitby

The present St Mary's Church, which was completed in 1896, was designed by Mr Walter H Brierly of York. Our 5 bells were hung in 1901, together with our Ellacombe frame which is installed, together with the church clock, in the tower, beneath the bell chamber. The ropes from the frame operate the clappers inside each bell. Independently, a network of rods and levers from the clock to the clappers on the outside of each bell ring the Westminster chimes. We ring our bells regularly for services in a simple sequence. The tenor bell has an additional rope to enable it to be rung from the vestry on the ground floor, where it is particularly convenient to toll for funerals.

The photograph shows Goathland's steel frame, made by bellfounders Taylor and Co of Loughborough, measuring 27 inches wide by 32 inches high, with pulleys, ropes, and the winding squares of the ratchet tensioners.

The movable handle is shown on the square of the tenor bell rope. While five bells is a relatively unusual number for an ordinary ring, it is dictated here by the chiming scheme, in this instance Cambridge Quarters, perhaps better known as Westminster Chimes. Though often in the key of E major, the bells at Goathland are actually in A major.

Our village is familiar to many for its use as the location of 'Aidensfield' in the Yorkshire Television series 'Hearbeat'. In one episode, most of which was filmed at our church, a team of six ringers were filmed ringing a peal of 8 swinging bells - they were clearly not ours!

# St Helens Parish Church, Wheldrake

Originally we had three bells hung for full circle ringing they came from the previous church which was replace with a new one in 1779. They were from 1640, 1658 and 1659 and were rung traditionally until they were silenced in 1914. When they came to ring them after the first world war the woodwork was in such a poor state that they couldn't be used.

As a war memorial by public subscription they raised enough to install three static bells and an Ellacombe Chiming apparatus was bought from Taylors of Loughbrough in 1920. Its recorded in a press cutting that the ringer Mr Beilby could now ring the six bells on his own.

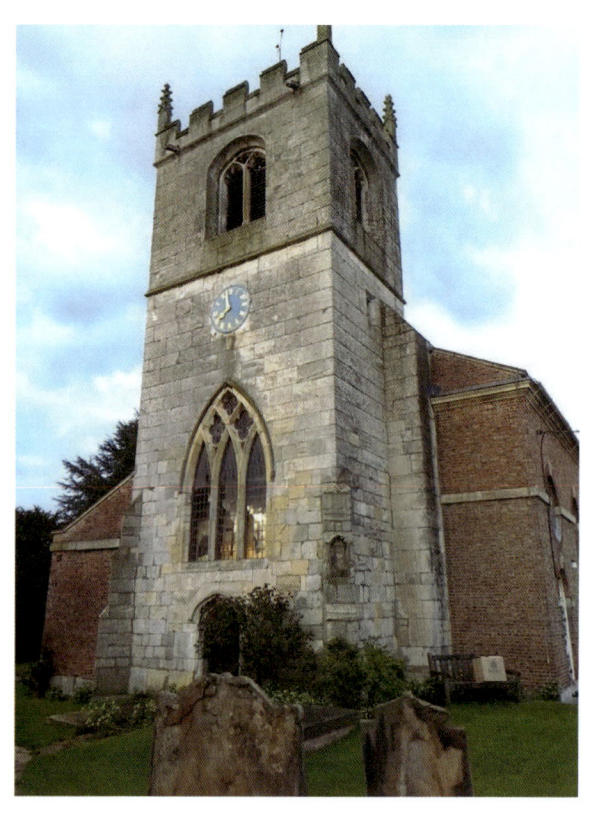

The bells were not in tune and could only be pattern rung. In 1998 a gift of a bell (Taylors 1988) was made, which brought them in tune and we were then able to ring tunes (we have 150 six note tunes and still adding to them).

The bells are rung each evening at 6.30pm. Whites of Appleton have been commissioned to renovate the whole system this year to keep it in good order.

*Paul Botting*

# St James the Great, Baldersby St James

The Church of St James was designed by the eminent Victorian Architect, William Butterfield, built by Mr R H Norris of London, and funded by William Henry Dawnay, 7th Viscount Downe. It was consecrated in 1857 and is Grade 1 Listed.

Mounted on a cast iron frame some eighty feet above the ground, the slender tower contains a ring of eight bells. Within the porch there is a door which, when opened, reveals a spiral stone stairway which leads to the ringing chamber and the bells themselves.

According to the Ripon and Richmond Chronicle dated 3 October 1857 reporting on the consecration and opening of the Church "there swung therein (the tower) eight glorious bells whose melodious tones would forever and a day assent and maintain the skill of one Master Taylor of Loughborough the founder thereof"

Unfortunately the mismatch of the slender tower, with an internal measurement of eleven feet by twelve feet, overloaded with bells weighing some six tons and too heavy for the tower, meant that the bells have been rarely rung as intended – that is full circle. On more than one occasion those ringers that tried are reported to have fled the tower in terror on account of its movement and the noise generated by the bell clappers striking the surrounding masonry.

Eventually discretion became the better part of valour and the church authorities at the time decided, in the late 1870's, to dispense with the eight bell ringers and their ropes and install an Ellacombe Chiming System. The system, put in place by Mr J R Jerram of Spalding, Lincolnshire, was very basic and lacked a ratchet and pawl system to adjust the ropes making the bells difficult to play.

Mr Butterfield was made fully aware of the potential overload and the possible consequences before the tower and spire were constructed but chose to ignore Mr Taylors concerns. Perhaps he was mindful of the instructions given by his patron, the Viscount Downe, who, when he placed the order with John Taylor, said "Let them be a good peal and don't spare the metal!" *Tim Helps*

## St Wilfrid's Burnsall

Nestling in the curve of the River Wharfe, St Wilfrid's lies towards the northern end of the village of Burnsall.

St Wilfrid's history goes right back to its foundation by St Wilfrid of Ripon before 700AD. Although most of the building has been rebuilt over the years, there are parts that go back many centuries. The font dates from an original Norman church, and the current Lady Chapel in the South Chantry was built in the twelfth century. The Tower and western portion of the church were built during the reign of Henry VIII (1509 - 1547).

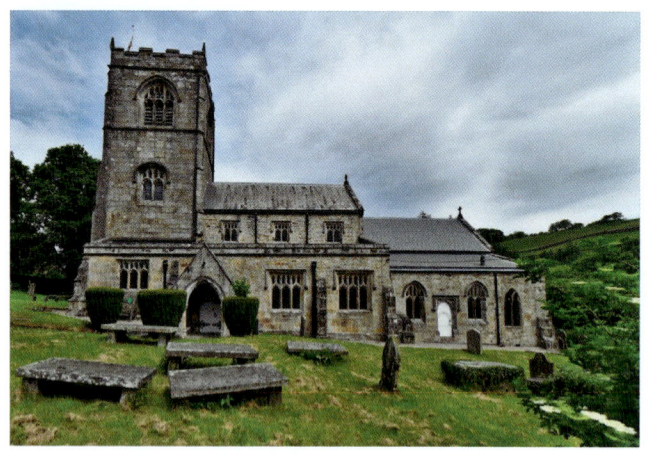

Photo Courtesy Michael Garlick; licensed for reuse under the Creative Commons Attribution-Share Alike 2.0 Generic licence

The Church has recently been used in the filming of the latest TV coverage of "All Creatures Great and Small".

St Wilfrid's is fortunate enough to be one of the approximately 400 Churches in the UK, and roughly 40 worldwide, to have Ellacombe chimes. They are now almost in working order after not being used for many, many years. This is thanks to the expertise of a villager Mr Jack Tinker, encouraged by organist and PCC member Ed Williams.

*Edwin Williams*

Photo courtesy John Clark

# NORTHAMPTONSHIRE
## St Giles Church, Desborough

Desborough Ellacombe apparatus is attached to 8 bells and located upstairs in the ringing room. When the bells were rehung in 2007 we made sure the Ellacombes were returned to working order. They have mostly been used for playing carols at christmas.

While we have been unable to ring during lockdown they have been used when services have been held in the church, with the ringers operating a rota.

# NORTHUMBERLAND
## Holy Trinity, Whitfield

Holy Trinity Whitfield is part of the Allen Valleys group of churches. At 750 feet above sea level, it is surrounded by extraordinarily beautiful upland country with a murmuring brook and fields of lambs in Spring. There is harsh winter weather but a main road through the village offers easy access at all times.

The church was built in 1860 and was the gift of Mrs Anne Jane Blackett-Ord in memory of her uncle William Ord from whom she had inherited the Whitfield Estate. The original Parish Church was partially dismantled in order to build Holy Trinity but it was also constructed using local stone. It has the tallest stone spire in rural Northumberland and used to be known as the Cathedral of the West Allen Valley.

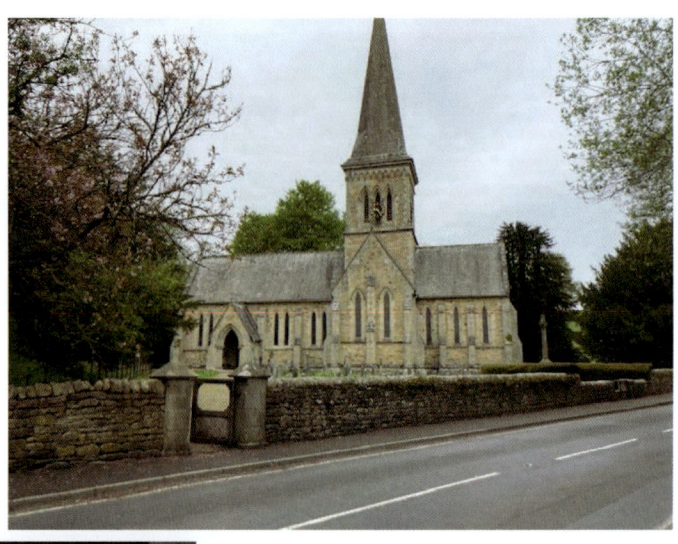

The Carillon was installed in 1978 to commemorate the late wife of JC Blackett-Ord, Elisabeth, who had died the year before. It was made by John Taylor and Co of Loughborough. It is situated in the vestry and can be played by anyone proficient on the piano. It has a particularly appealing ring and is versatile enough to accommodate tunes as well as peels...a lovely sound ringing out across the valley.

*Sarah Blackett-Ord*

## OXFORDSHIRE
## St. Leonard's Church, Waterstock

The village of Waterstock can be traced back to Saxon times, and it remains a tiny community, clustered around its church and manor house. The current church dates largely from its 15th-century rebuilding. From about 1550 the tower began to acquire significant bells, gradually augmented by the Lords of the Manor, notably the Croke and Ashhurst families, whose memorials adorn the church walls and windows.

During subsequent centuries these locally-cast bells sprouted wheels and fittings for full-circle ringing, as was becoming common. But when in 1888 the augmention to six bells became a reality, something prevented their increase to a fully ringing peal (probably concern for stresses on the masonry), and they were hung 'dead': in other words, their headstocks were bolted down to the frame members.

This meant they had to be sounded by chiming hammers, and so an Ellacombe apparatus was installed. This is still of the original pattern, whereby the ropes are tensioned simply by tying them to a wooden rail.

The 1888 casting and recasting was carried out by the Croydon foundry of Gillett & Co. (later Gillett and Johnston), the three old bells becoming the trebles, and the new tenor weighing 7 cwt. 3 qr. 21 lb.

# The Orthodox Church of St Nicholas the Wonderworker, Marston, Oxford

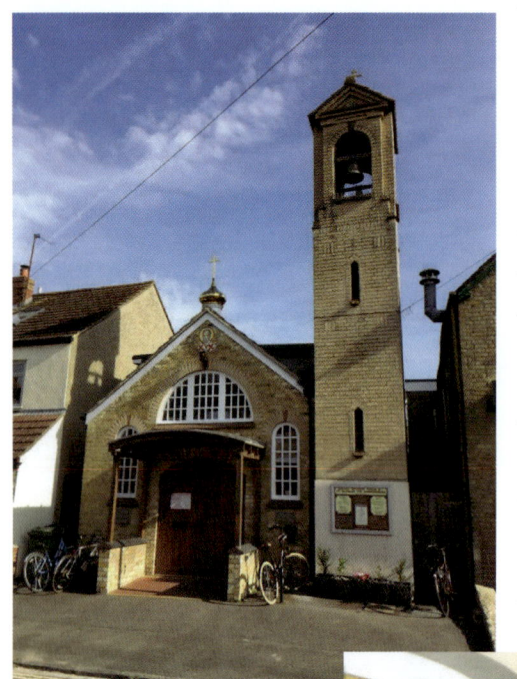

The Ellacombe Chimes frame in the Orthodox Church of St Nicholas the Wonderworker in Oxford was installed as recently as 2012 by Whites of Appleton Ltd., who hung the bells and carried out the design and installation of the frame. We believe ours to be the only Ellacombe mechanism in use in an Orthodox church in the UK, and possibly in the world.

The building, which dates from 1910, was originally the first Anglican mission church for New Marston, Oxford, but was closed for worship following the construction of a new parish church, St Michael and All Angels, in the 1950s. The one original bell was transferred to the new church at that time. After many years in a derelict condition, the building was purchased by Oxford's Russian Orthodox parish, who carried out a full renovation of the building, It was consecrated as an Orthodox Church in September 2010.

In 2012, the church received a gift of four specially cast bells from the Diocese of Voronezh in Russia, a city long famous for its bell foundries. The bells range in weight from 60 to 10 kgs, and each is cast with an icon of a saint connected with the church.

Russian church bells are usually chimed, rather than rung, The ringer of ringers will perform sometimes highly complex patterns of chimes in various rhythmic arrangements, each arrangement, or zvon, being used to mark different feasts, special occasions, services or seasons in the church year. *Fr. Stephen Platt*

## St Michael at the North Gate, Oxford

Built before 1060 as part of the Anglo-Saxon fortifications of Oxford, the tower watched over the northern entrance to the city. The upper windows retain their original appearance and indicate that the tower also served as a belfry. St Michael's church was mentioned in the Domesday Book (1086), but the present structure dates from the thirteenth century. The tower was incorporated into this new church and in the fifteenth century an arch was inserted opening up the lower levels to the rest of the building.

For much of its history, the church tower was obscured by adjacent buildings, in particular the North Gate and above it the Bocardo prison. The most celebrated inmates of the Bocardo were Archbishop Thomas Cranmer, the architect of the English Reformation, and Bishops Hugh Latimer and Nicholas Ridley. Imprisoned for their Protestant beliefs, following Mary I's restoration of Catholicism, the bishops were burnt for heresy in October 1555 and the archbishop the following year. The North Gate and Bocardo were pulled down in 1772 and in the early twentieth century the last remaining building adjoining the tower was demolished.

The tower's bells are mentioned in an early fourteenth century inquest. A student, Robert de Honiton had wanted to help ring on New Year's Eve 1301 but had fallen to his death. Of the current bells, the oldest four were cast in 1668 by Robert Keene at Woodstock. Two further bells were cast by the Rudhall family at Gloucester in 1708 and 1755. At the end of the nineteenth century, serious cracks in the structure of the Saxon tower brought an end to bell ringing at St Michael's. The Ellacombe chiming frame, however, means that the bells can still be heard across Oxford.

*Professor Andrew Spicer*

## St. Leonard's Church, Waterstock

The village of Waterstock can be traced back to Saxon times, and it remains a tiny community, clustered around its church and manor house. The current church dates largely from its 15th-century rebuilding. From about 1550 the tower began to acquire significant bells, gradually augmented by the Lords of the Manor, notably the Croke and Ashhurst families, whose memorials adorn the church walls and windows.

During subsequent centuries these locally-cast bells sprouted wheels and fittings for full-circle ringing, as was becoming common. But when in 1888 the augmention to six bells became a reality, something prevented their increase to a fully ringing peal (probably concern for stresses on the masonry), and they were hung 'dead': in other words, their headstocks were bolted down to the frame members.

This meant they had to be sounded by chiming hammers, and so an Ellacombe apparatus was installed. This is still of the original pattern, whereby the ropes are tensioned simply by tying them to a wooden rail.

The 1888 casting and recasting was carried out by the Croydon foundry of Gillett & Co. (later Gillett and Johnston), the three old bells becoming the trebles, and the new tenor weighing 7 cwt. 3 qr. 21 lb.

138

# SOUTH GLOUCESTERSHIRE
## St Mary's - Bitton

An ancient church of national importance, St Mary's has probably been a site of worship since Roman times and possibly predates the establishment of the English church under St Augustine. The church is situated close between the river Avon and the old Roman Road, the Via Julia, and recent archaeology has revealed stones and ceramic shards from the Roman period in the church's foundations. The existing church, dedicated to St Mary the Virgin, dates from around 500AD and was extended and refashioned during the Norman period. Both Saxon and Norman features remain, including sections of a giant Saxon stone Rood (probably demolished during the Reformation) as well as Norman doorways and windows.

Until 1936 the St Mary's ring was of six bells and they were hung on wooden frames. The six bells were restored and rehung; two new treble bells were added.

At Bitton we have the original Ellacombe Chimes. The Rev. H.T. Ellacombe, Vicar of Bitton from 1817 to 1850, wanted some means of enabling the bells to be rung by one person.

Ellacombe's own words in his history of Bitton, published in 1881, Ellacombe writes:

> "In the basement of the tower is a manual within a case for chiming the bells for services by means of a hammer striking the inside of the bell. This was set up in 1822. The method was suggested to me by Sam Watts, a clever workman, and is supposed to be the first thing of that sort. Since that time the contrivance has been set up in about 200 towers."

The Rev. H.T.Ellacombe was Vicar from 1817 to 1850 and was then succeeded by his son, Henry, who was Vicar until his death in 1916. Between them they served the Parish for a total of 99 years.

## SURREY
# St Philomena's Catholic High School for Girls founded by the Daughters of the Cross, Carshalton

The school was founded in 1893 by the Daughters of the Cross, whose foundress was Blessed Marie Thérèse. The Ellacombe Chime frame at St Philomena's school is located in the Chapel which was built between 1899-1900. The school now has approximately 1450 students with 25 students who are part of the Bell Ringing society which was re-established in 2018. After a long silence, the eight bells in the chapel tower were cleaned and fixed. The apparatus was jammed and needed a good clean as some of the ropes were unable to pull the hammer to hit the bell.

Our bells are hung 'dead' and do not move. The bells in the tower are marked by Gillett and Johnston of Croydon cast in 1930. With the help of a local volunteer the bells were restored. Although they all now work, some more work needs to be done in order to get a slightly better sound on the two lightest bells, but students can once again begin to learn how to bellring. Students have learnt how to ring rounds and various tunes such as Queens, Tittums and Kings.

The bells are rung weekly, before Mass on a Tuesday morning, Wednesday practice at lunchtime, memorial days, feast days, Advent and at Christmas when students learn how to play Christmas Carols.

For the Chime Around the World' event in June students are taking part in a fun 'striking competition' followed by ringing at noon and a picnic in the school grounds.

A special thanks to the Surrey Association of Bellringers as well as St Mary's Catholic Church in Clapham which has provided music and training. *Thomas Newman. Assistant Headteacher of St Philomena's.*

## St Mathew's, Surbiton

St Matthew's is a Grade II listed Victorian church, built in 1875 at the expense of William Coulthurst, senior partner of Coutts Bank. The spire is 53m high, topping Nelson's Column by 1 metre!

When the church was built a chime system with a set of eight hemispherical bells was installed (see picture) which enable a single ringer to play a full octave in the key of E flat. The largest hemisphere weighs 4.5 cwt. (nearly 230 kilograms.) The hemispheres are hung in a field-gate frame on 6 levels and chimed from an Ellacombe manual. John Warner of London's Cripplegate supplied the system, and it had been in constant.

In 2017 significant deterioration of the tower was discovered. The stonework was severely damaged including the window mullions in the belfry. A major restoration project was undertaken, completing in 2020.

During the restoration, the entire chime system was overhauled by John Taylor & Co of Loughborough, one of the last remaining foundries capable of such work. The eight hemispheres were removed for restoration at the foundry, and reinstalled in the closing weeks of the project. They ring aloud again.

St Matthew's is keen for the restored system to be fully appreciated; it has installed CCTV to help to engage the community to see the system at work. This increases accessibility as the steps up the tower are incredibly steep! A replica bell-frame has been constructed to explain the mechanism of the Ellacombe system, and enable youngsters to try chime ringing, at ground level.

The tower also houses a large single service bell which bears an inscription dating it to 1734. This bell was 'recycled' by the original bell-founders when a church in Kenilworth decommissioned their existing peal, no doubt to give it a brand new home.

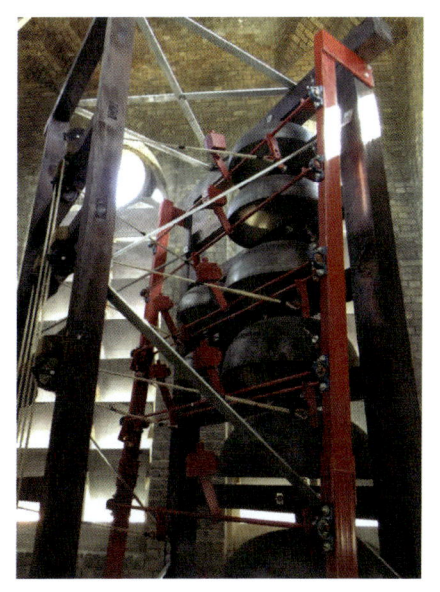

## WARWICKSHIRE
## St James the Great Church, Snitterfield

The bell tower at St James the Great, Snitterfield, contains a grand ring of six bells, which hang level with the louvre windows. The bells were last fully rehung and restored in 1887. A new oak and cast bellframe was installed and all new bell fittings put in place. In 1947, a partial rehang and overhaul was carried out.

A survey carried out in September 2018 revealed that, while our lovely bells had been very well looked after, some major work was required to ensure that they—and the bellringers—could continue to herald many key events, national and local. Apart from the regular Sunday morning call to worship, the bells announce weddings, funerals, Christmas, New Year and join in with national ringing for such events as Armistice Day and the Millennium.

*The workforce at the recent restoration*

A Bells Restoration Appeal was launched to raise the necessary £50K+ and, despite the pandemic and lockdowns, work was carried out by John Taylor & Co of Loughborough. This is the same company that carried out the major works in 1887. At the same time, the decision was made to update and restore the Ellacombe, which had proved so useful when bellringers were scarce and helps to make our bell tower special. We now have a number of new, developing ringers, some of whom are keen to learn how to ring the Ellacombe, and also receive visiting ringers who test their skills in our tower.

An Open Day is being held on 26th June to celebrate the Ellacombe bi-centenary and dedicate the newly restored Bells of St James. An electronic time capsule to include some original scores for the Ellacombe will be placed in the Bell Tower to ensure the tradition continues. *Sue Lambert*

## St Mary's Warwick

During the recent periods of lockdown, the Ellacombe Chimes in Warwickshire have provided an alternative to full circle ringing. The apparatus in St Mary's Warwick was rarely used, until 2020, since when it has sounded most weeks to remind communities of the continuing presence of the church and its bells.

St Mary's have 10 bells, the heaviest of which weighs 24 cwt, in the key of D. There were 5 bells in the 16th century, and in the mid 17th Century they were augmented to 8. All the bells were destroyed in the great fire of Warwick in 1694. At the start of the 18th century 8 new bells were cast by Rudhall, a Gloucester bell founder, and very soon they were augmented to a ring of 10. Thomas Mears, a bell founder working in the Whitechapel foundry, then recast the tenor bell in 1814. The ring was completely overhauled in 1901 by John Taylors of Loughborough and 6 of the bells were recast. The current ring of bells contains 6 Taylor bells, 3 from Rudhalls bells from 1701 and the tenor recast from 1814.

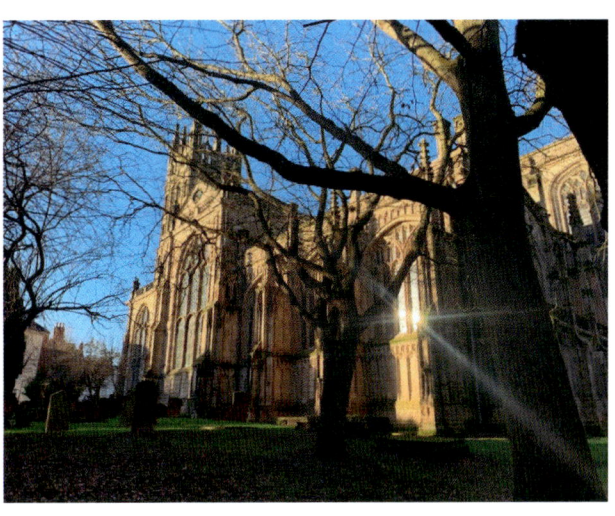

*St Mary's Warwick, Christmas Morning*

Prior to Sunday Service ringing, the Ellacombe can be heard ringing well known hymns. Carols are played at Christmas, but also change ringing methods can often be heard. The tenor of the Ellacombe is sometimes used for mid week funerals.

On Saturday 26th June, the Ellacombe will ring out over Warwick. There will be a combination of tunes and changes to entertain the people of the town.

*Christopher Mew, a well-known ringer with the St Mary's Warwick Ellacombe.*

Annie Hall

## St Peter's Catholic Church, Leamington Spa

St Peter's Catholic Church in Dormer Place in Leamington Spa was completed in 1864, replacing an older catholic church in another part of the town. The tower was added in 1877-1878, financed by Miss France, who contributed generously to the building of the church itself. Unfortunately the church was burnt down in 1883 but was rebuilt in red brick with stone dressings in 1884. There was a pyramidal spire on top of the tower initially but this was removed for safety reasons in about 1958.

The slender brick tower is connected to the main church via a low entrance corridor and it therefore gets little support from the body of the church. The bells are hung high in the tower and consequently, when the bells are rung full circle, there is considerable tower movement which means that even the most experienced ringers can have difficulty handling them. The tower movement can be felt even at the lowest stages of the tower.

Originally there were 6 bells in the tower, cast by Thomas Blews of Birmingham in 1877. These were replaced by Taylor's of Loughborough in 1905, the ring being made up to 8 bells hung on 2 levels in the key of F$^\sharp$. The Ellacombe chiming apparatus, situated in the ringing room, was added in 1955 by Taylor's, as full circle ringing of the bells was at that time deemed to be unviable due to the tower movement. Measurements taken in the 1980's showed that ringing the bells full circle was possible for short periods and they are now rung, largely by ringers from other churches, for the important feast days in the Catholic calendar. The Ellacombe apparatus is used mainly for playing tunes after weddings and other specially selected occasions. Although the tunes are restricted by just a major scale there are plenty of possibilities e.g. a slightly revised version of the "Match of the Day" theme was requested by one couple after they heard it at a previous wedding they attended. *Simon Rogers*

# WEST SUSSEX
## St Wilfrid's Haywards Heath

Haywards Heath began to develop as an urban settlement in the mid nineteenth century with the arrival of the London & Brighton railway. Anglican services started being held in Haywards Heath in 1856, rather fittingly above a carpenter's shop near the new railway station. Before long, plans for a church were underway and St Wilfrid's was dedicated in 1865. The tower was built with the capacity for a ring of eight bells, although it appears that finances became challenging. Instead of installing tower bells, a set of Harrington's Tubular Chimes (supplied by Messrs. Harrington, Latham & Co. Coventry), was purchased for £155. These were installed and then dedicated on 12 October (St Wilfrid's day), 1888.

The bells were paid for as follows:
Bell 1 - Miss Marion Lindsay Smith Elfinsward £10
Bell 2 - Mrs Hannan, Lucastes £12
Bell 3 - Miss Annie Cooper, In Memoriam }
Bell 4 - Miss Jane Cooper, In Memoriam }
Bell 5 - Mrs S Cooper, Fair Lawn}
Bell 6 - Mr S Cooper, Fair Lawn }    £67
Bell 7 - General Subscriptions }
Bell 8 - General Subscriptions }
Bell 9 - General Subscriptions }    £45
Bell 10 - Thomas Astley Maberly   £21

The bells have been rung since their dedication as a call to service with a recent break between 1996 and 2012 when they were rung only for weddings. The bells were overhauled and rehung by Messrs Gillett & Johnston (Croydon) in 1950, and further work was undertaken by the Whitechapel Bell Foundry in 1987. In August 2018 Nicholson Engineering transported the bells to their workshop in Bridport for restoration. Because of cracks discovered in three of the bells which needed specialist welding, it was February 2019 before the bells were re-installed in the tower. *Jill Garraway with photos by Melvyn Walmsley*

## St Bartholomew, Rogate

The church is situated in the village of Rogate in West Sussex and within the South Downs National Park. The church is a designated Grade 1 building and the unbroken list of Vicars goes back to 1222.

St Bartholomew's has a complex building history, starting in the 12th century. The main structure comprises a mixture of local sandstone (Greensand) and Purbeck with Bath Stone dressings. The oldest visible portion of the building is a round Norman arch at the east end of the north arcade in the Nave, built in about 1150. Most of the other arches in the Nave date from the 13th century. There is further work from the 13th, 14th and 15th centuries in the Chancel and Sanctuary.

Until 1874, the timber tower, dated about 1330, stood between what are now the two central arches of the Nave arcades. The church, which had become very dilapidated and dangerous, was extensively rebuilt and extended westwards. The timber tower was taken down piece by piece and rebuilt in its present position within a new stone casing at the base. The tower is the outstanding architectural feature of the church, and something of the splendour of the ancient Wealden oaks can be gauged from the size of its timbers.

The bell tower houses a ring of six bells in the key of F# from the smallest Treble (St Bartholomew) weighing over 2cwt to the Tenor (St Paul) weighing over 8cwt. They were all cast, lathe turned and hung by John Taylor & Co in 1904, the work completed on Christmas Eve 1904.

In 2014 an additional Sanctus bell was installed above the other bells to commemorate the Centenary of the Great War, with the names of the fallen from the village cast on the bell.

## U.K. SCOTLAND
## STIRLING AND FALKIRK
# Dunblane Cathedral

In 1907 Robert Younger KC offered to donate a new set of bells and clock to the recently restored Dunblane Cathedral. John Taylor & Co. of Loughborough offered several schemes:

- A ring of eight bells hung with ropes and wheels for change ringing and rung by a team of ringers,
- A carillon of 37 bells covering three chromatic octaves, operated by a "carillonneur" and used to play music with harmonies,
- A chime of eight bells hung stationery, sounded by moving hammers and operated by a single ringer to play simple melodies, with one additional bell hung with rope and wheel.

The latter option was chosen and on Monday 28th September 1908 the bells were first chimed when King Edward VII visited the Cathedral. The chime at Dunblane was unusual because the bells could be chimed by two independent systems; there was a "baton clavier" using wooden levers to operate clappers inside the bells as well as an Ellacombe chiming apparatus, more usually found in change ringing installations.

A chime was considered a better option as it put less strain on the tower and could be operated by one person rather than a team of ringers. Robert Younger must have been keen on the idea of change ringing because, when he died, in 1946 he left £2,500 to convert the chime into a ringing peal. The two lightest bells were recast, and the bells were rehung for change ringing in 1952. The bell already hung with a rope and wheel was retained giving a sharp 5th thus allowing a "middle six" to be rung. The Ellacombe mechanism was also retained.

The Dunblane Cathedral Society of Change Ringers was founded in 1975. There is a strong change ringing band but the Ellacombe is still used regularly to ring both hymns and changes.

*Judith Frye, Tower Captain*

## PEEBLESHIRE
## Peebles Old Parish Church, Peebles

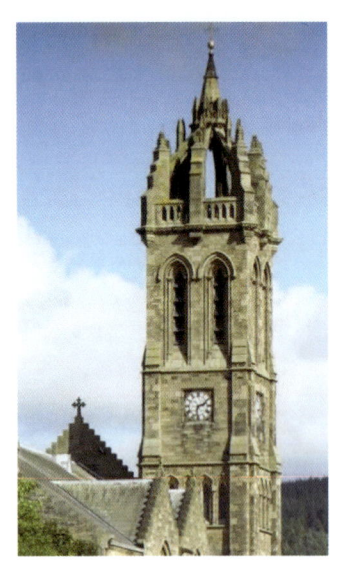

Our bells were made and installed by the firm of Taylor's of Loughborough, between the years 1939 and 1940. They were, of course, not rung until after the end of World War II.

There are 13 bells, which are hung 'dead': that is the bells don't swing but instead are stationary and are struck by a hammer. They are played by one person standing at a keyboard.

This type of arrangement is called a 'carillon' and is very common on the Continent. There are about half a dozen carillons in Scotland, including a very large one in Aberdeen. The keyboard is on the same level as the clock faces while the bells are housed in the floor above – the part which, when seen from outside, has the slatted windows.

From 1947 until his death in 1988, the bells were rung by Wilbert Whitie, an elder of the church and well-known local bookseller. After his death, a Bellringers Group was formed and consists of about a dozen people who take turns each Sunday to ring the bells.

The group, which is very enthusiastic, includes members from other churches in the town.

The donor of the bells was Dr Alfred Ernest Maylard. He was a well-known physician and the author of many medical books. He was also a founding member of the Scottish Mountaineering Club and was the author of the book 'Walks around Peebles'. He retired to live at Kingsmuir and died in Peebles in 1947, aged 92. He gifted the bells in memory of his wife.

*Anne Derrick*

148

# UK WALES
## CAERPHILLY
# St Martin's Church, Caerphilly

*Photo courtesy Jaggery: Attribution-ShareAlike 2.0 Generic (CC BY-SA 2.0)*

St Martin's Church in Caerphilly was constructed in the late 1870's to form the principal Church in the new Parish of Caerphilly, on the site of the former Capel Martin which had been a daughter Church in the Parish of Eglwysilan of which the Caerphilly area had been part. The tower was added in the late 1900's and a set of 8 bells with a 13 cwt. tenor installed by John Taylor & Co in 2010. The bells are considered to produce a particularly nice sound and the tenor bell is unusually a 'maiden' bell, i.e. no further fine tuning was required to the bell as cast. After a period when the bells had fallen into disuse a new band of ringers was formed in 1974, a number of whom remain part of the current band.

It is not known when the Ellacombe chiming apparatus was installed in the tower, though it is perhaps likely this would have been done at the time of installation of the bells. St Martin's is a popular Church for weddings and the ringing of bells on such occasions is normally done by chiming by trained younger members of the congregation for whom it forms a source of regular pocket money. The chiming apparatus also provides the highlight when from time to time various groups of mainly young people visit the tower and they are allowed to take it in turn to ring the chimes and provide sound which can be heard by local residents. The apparatus has been of further use at the time of writing this note when the chimes have been used to provide ringing for Church services at a time when restrictions as a result of the Covid-19 pandemic has prevented the provision of full circle ringing.

*Peter Jones*

# CARDIFF
## Llandaff Cathedral
10 bell Ellacombe

As far as is known the Ellacombe apparatus has been in almost continuous use since 1919 when the bells were augmented from 8 to 10; it was not modified when the new 12 were installed in 1992. The bells are in the Jasper Tower, not the spire.

There is a rota of 5 dependable people who chime before the 9 o'clock service on Sunday mornings. They have continued throughout the pandemic when normal ringing hasn't been possible.

The 12 bells are rung fully open before the 11 am service, for special services and some civic events.

*Pat Moore*

# CONWY
## St Cynbryd's Church, Llanddulas

St Cynbryd's Church was consecrated in 1869 and originally had two small "bell-shaped" bells but these were replaced in 1909 by a peal of 6 tubular bells made by Harrington, Latham & Co, Coventry, England. Two more bells, also by Harrington & Latham, were added in 1912. The bell tower is at the west end (left end in the photo) of the church, and the tower is very narrow and projects only a small distance above the church roof.

In 2010, after a number of years when the hammer mechanisms were inoperative due to corrosion and decayed fabric, the bells were restored. The bells had to be removed from their frame in the tower and lowered individually, and the dismantled frame pieces lowered after them, and everything taken away for restoration by John Taylor & Co, Bellfounders, Bellhangers & Carillon Builders, Loughborough, UK.

When the bells are assembled in the tower, they are neither visible nor easily accessible. Therefore, when the bells were restored, they were assembled and working on the floor of the church for a week, as shown in the photograph. The largest bell, at the back on the right, is 2.06m long and weighs about 142kg. All the bells are bronze. The whole structure was then dismantled and hauled piece by piece up the narrow vertical inside of the tower to be re-assembled.

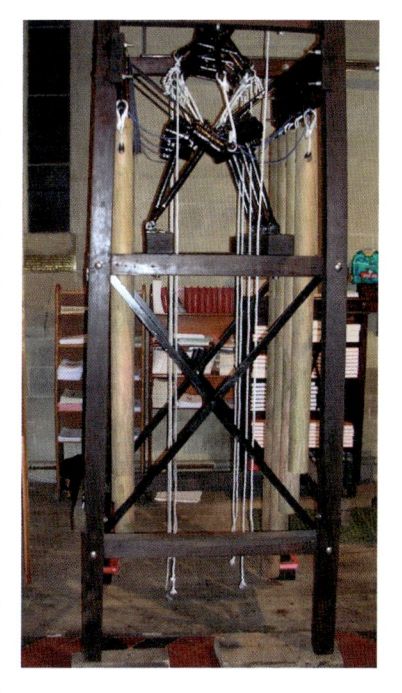

The picture of the chime frame at the bottom of the tower shows how confined the space is with only enough room for one person. In the centre of the picture behind the pull-ropes, a horizontal iron rung step is visible. There is a series of these steps all the way up the tower, and through two trap doors, to give access to the bells at the top. *Brian Bell*

# VALE OF GLAMORGAN
## St Andrew's, Dinas Powys

St Andrew's is a Grade II* listed building that sits within an ancient churchyard in the Vale of Glamorgan. A stone building first appeared on the site in the C12 and the church was expanded and added to right up until the C20. The tower and the porch date from the C15. The tower is a 4 storeyed structure containing 5 bells cast by William Evans who worked from a foundry owned by his father in Chepstow.

Installed in 1747 by Rector Nathaniel Wells, they bear the inscription:

> 'Come let us ring for Church and King,
> Peace and good neighbourhood.
> William Evans cast us all 1747
> John Gwillim and John Jenkins Churchwardens
> The Rev. Mr Nathaniel Wells, Rector '

The Nave and chancel underwent an understated Victorian restoration when a painted ceiling in the chancel was completed by General H. H. Lee and his wife in 1885. The east window was installed along with the gift of a brass eagle lectern and a carved oak reredos. The interior of the church then remained largely unaltered until the need for extensive work in the late 1990s.

In 1919 the bell ropes were replaced and the Parish magazine article of the PCC meeting reported that 'parishioners are delighted once again to hear the sweet bells of S. Andrews calling them to worship and prayer' By the 1950s money was tight, and repairs to the bell frame were too expensive for the PCC to undertake. As the bells were then in too dangerous a state to be swung, the PCC reported on a piece of equipment that could be used to chime the bells and the Ellacombe chiming apparatus was installed. The Ellacombe is in use every Sunday and on other special occasions and open days    *Judith Anderson*

# St Augustine's, Penarth

The church itself was completed in 1866 having been designed by the famous Victorian architect, William Butterfield. The interior of the church has been described as one of his best "polychromatic churches", the ringing chamber, however, is yellow Bath stone and grey Lias limestone, overpainted with blue and grey.

There were originally six bells in the saddleback tower. The augmentation to eight was in 1935. The Ellacombe has apparatus for all eight bells, there is no apparent date on it, but it must have been augmented or installed after this time.

It is not currently in use partly as the Tower has a large enough number of ringers to consistently cover Services. Further, being the highest coastal feature in the area, the Tower is prone to degradation by salt water and damp. Some of the hammer mechanisms have rusted and it has had to have some maintenance to free up the pulleys – we hope in time for the bicentenary.

*Helen Kerbey*

Printed in Great Britain
by Amazon